Digging Out of the Great Depression
Federal Programs at Work In and Around Birmingham

For Reference

Not to be taken from this room

Birmingham Historical Society

TRUSSVILLE PUBLIC LIBRARY
201 PARKWAY DRIVE
TRUSSVILLE, AL 35173
(205) 655-2022

Library of Congress Cataloging-in-Publication Data

Digging out of the Great Depression : federal programs at work in and around Birmingham / edited by Julius E. Linn, Jr., Katherine M. Tipton, and Marjorie L. White. -- Original limited ed.
   p. cm.
 Includes bibliographical references and index.
 ISBN 978-0-943994-35-2 (alk. paper)
 1. New Deal, 1933-1939--Alabama--Birmingham Region. 2. New Deal, 1933-1939--Alabama--Birmingham Region--Pictorial works. 3. Birmingham Region (Ala.)--Economic conditions--20th century. 4. Birmingham Region (Ala.)--Economic conditions--20th century--Pictorial works. 5. Birmingham Region (Ala.)--Social conditions--20th century. 6. Birmingham Region (Ala.)--Social conditions--20th century--Pictorial works. 7. Public welfare--Alabama--Birmingham Region--History--20th century. 8. Birmingham Region (Ala.)--Intellectual life--20th century. 9. Art and state--Alabama--Birmingham Region--History--20th century. 10. Federal government--United States--History--20th century. I. Linn, Julius E. II. Tipton, Katherine M., 1959- III. White, Marjorie Longenecker. IV. Birmingham Historical Society.
 HC108.B6D54 2010
 330.9761'781062--dc22
                           2010027417

ORIGINAL LIMITED EDITION
Copyright 2010 by Birmingham Historical Society

Birmingham Historical Society
One Sloss Quarters
Birmingham, Alabama 35222
www.bhistorical.org

This book is published in conjunction with the exhibitions *Digging Out of the Great Depression–Federal Programs At Work* (2009) and *Murals, Murals On the Wall, 1929–1939–Our Story Through Art in Public Places* (2010), organized by the Birmingham Historical Society and the Birmingham Public Library, with the financial support of the Daniel Foundation of Alabama and the Alabama Humanities Foundation, a state program of the National Endowment for the Humanities. The latter exhibition is made possible in part by the Alabama Cooperative Extension System and the Jule Collins Smith Museum of Fine Art, Auburn, Alabama.

ISBN 978-0-943994-35-2
Printed in China

FRONT COVER PHOTOGRAPHS:
"Steel mill and workers' houses. Birmingham, Alabama."
Photograph by Walker Evans, 1936. Courtesy the Library of Congress Farm Security Administration–Office of War Information Photograph Collection (LOC-FSA).

Playground Supervision, ACIPCO Park.
Photograph, 1930s. Courtesy Birmingham Public Library Department of Archives and Manuscripts (BPL Archives).

Jefferson Hospital–Now Jefferson Tower, UAB Medical Center.
Photograph, circa 1940. Courtesy BPL Archives.

Vulcan Monument in Vulcan Park, atop Red Mountain.
Photograph by O. V. Hunt, circa 1939. Courtesy BPL Archives.

BACK COVER PHOTOGRAPHS:
"Digging dirt used in rammed earth construction near Birmingham, Alabama."
Photograph by Thomas Hibben Jr., March 1937. Courtesy LOC-FSA.

Agriculture Moves Onward, Historical Panorama of Alabama Agriculture.
John Augustus Walker. Mural panel (one of ten), tempera on canvas, 1939. Created for the Alabama Cooperative Extension Service Exhibition, Alabama State Fair, Birmingham, October 1939. Courtesy Alabama Cooperative Extension Ssytem.

Clinic in the Slossfield Hospital.
Photograph courtesy UAB Archives, University of Alabama at Birmingham.

TITLE PAGE PHOTOGRAPH:
"Digging dirt used in rammed earth construction near Birmingham, Alabama."
Photograph by Thomas Hibben Jr., March 1937. Courtesy LOC-FSA.

Designer: Scott Fuller

Table of Contents

Acknowledgments iv

Preface v

Introduction ix

Chapter One
Alphabet Agencies 1

Chapter Two
Putting the First 15,000 to Work: The Civil Works Administration (CWA) 4

Chapter Three
Roosevelt's Tree Army: The Civilian Conservation Corps (CCC) 18
      A Great and Lasting Good: CCC Structures in Alabama Parks 34

Chapter Four
Better Housing for Industrial Workers: Subsistence Homesteads and Public Housing 38
      Documenting Working and Living Conditions 40
      Palmerdale Homesteads 50
      Greenwood Homesteads 52
      Moving Out and In 54
      Mount Olive Homesteads 56
      Rammed Earth Houses 58
      Slagheap Village–Cahaba Village at Trussville 64
      Other Housing Ventures 66

Chapter Five
Jobs for the Jobless: The Works Progress Administration (WPA) 72

Chapter Six
Creating a City Beautiful: WPA Beautification Efforts 84

Chapter Seven
Artists on Relief: A New Deal for the Arts 88

Chapter Eight
On Stage: The Federal Theatre Project (FTP) 104

Chapter Nine
Digging Up the Past: Advances in Archaeology 108

Chapter Ten
Recording Our Heritage: The Historic American Buildings Survey (HABS) 114

Chapter Eleven
Built to Last: A Legacy in Stone at Birmingham Parks 120

Index 131

Acknowledgments

Designer
Scott Fuller

Photographs of Surviving Murals and Structures
Marc Bondarenko
Brian Rushing
Frank Jefferson Tombrello
Pam Venz's Birmingham-Southern College 2003 Jan-Term Studio Students: Adam Colbert, Charles Horn, Annette Kittrell, Jamie Neal, Andrew Ryan, and Booth Wilson

Birmingham Historical Society
Officers: Pat Camp, Wayne Hester, Julius Linn Jr., Carol Slaughter, Rick Sprague, Katie Tipton, and Marjorie White
Trustees assisting with this book and associated exhibitions: Regina Ammon, Kaydee Erdreich Breman, Harold Goings, Sallie Lee, Carolanne Roberts, Brian Rushing, and Jim Strickland

Birmingham Public Library
For support of research and for sponsoring the two exhibitions associated with this book, *Digging Out of the Great Depression–Federal Programs At Work* (2009) and *Murals, Murals On the Wall, 1929-1939–Our Story Through Art in Public Places* (2010):
Renee Blaylock, Director
Angela Fischer Hall and Pamela Lyons, Associate Directors
Don Veasey, Curator of Photographs; Gigi Gowdy and Yolanda Valentin, Archival Assistants, Archives Department
Ben Petersen, Southern History Department
Government Documents Department
Jim Baggett, Kelsey Bates, Frank Golden, Sandi Lee, Melinda Shelton, and Linda Wilson
Elizabeth Swift, Jefferson County Library Cooperative, Integrated Library Systems Administrator

Alabama Cooperative Extension System, Auburn, Alabama
Gaines Smith, Director
C. Bruce Dupree, Art Specialist
Sallie Lee, Jefferson County Agent
Carol Whatley, Communications and Marketing Director

Alabama Department of Archives and History
Martha McLemore

Birmingham Botanical Gardens Library Archives and Rare Book Room
Jason Kirby, Archivist

Montgomery Museum of Fine Arts, Montgomery, Alabama
Alice Carter, Librarian; Pam Bransford, Registrar

Jule Collins Smith Museum of Fine Art, Auburn, Alabama
Marilyn Laufer, Director

UAB Archives, University of Alabama at Birmingham
Tim L. Pennycuff, Assistant Professor and University Archivist, University of Alabama Museums

Moundville Archaeological Park, Moundville, Alabama
William F. Bomar, Director

University of Alabama Museums, Tuscaloosa, Alabama
Mary J. Bade, Director of Museum Collections
Mike Dressler, Collections Assistant
Eugene Futato, Senior Archaeologist and Deputy Director

U.S. Forest Service, Montgomery, Alabama
Robert Pasquill Jr., Archaeologist

Special Appreciation
John Bertalan; Birmingham Board of Education; Graham Boettcher, Birmingham Museum of Art; Jeff Brasher, Boy Scouts of America; Enrico Caporaso, Postmaster, Montevallo Post Office; Patrick Cather; Leslie R. Collins, Tallassee, Tennessee; Mildred Crain; John Davis, Birmingham Zoo; Leah Donnelly, Special Collections and Archives, George Mason University; Veronica Fisher, Special Collections and Archives, George Mason University; Steve Gilmer, What's On Second?; Jane Goings; Clarice Goodwin; Shirley G. Graham, Woodlawn High School; Beth Hunter, Gardendale Historical Society; Lynn B. Williams Katz, Auburn, Alabama; Maria Kennedy, Daniel Foundation of Alabama; Nora Lewis, Georgia Historical Society; Mary Ann Martin, Martin Advertising, Inc.; Jeff Meadows, Woodlawn High School; Patti Mulock, Belleair, Florida; Patty Pendleton, Birmingham Zoo; Susan Perry, Alabama Humanities Foundation; Julee Potter, Davis Architects, Inc.; Angelo Price, Bessemer Park and Recreation Department; Jordan H. Prince, Locust Valley, New York; Bob Stewart, Alabama Humanities Foundation; Ed Young, Postmaster, Fairfield Post Office

Collections
Alabama Department of Archives and History
Department of Archives and Manuscripts, Birmingham Public Library
Farm Security Administration–Office of War Information Photograph Collection, Library of Congress
Federal Theatre Project Collection, Special Collections and Archives, George Mason University Libraries
Franklin D. Roosevelt Presidential Library and Museum
Georgia Historical Society, Savannah, Georgia
Historic American Buildings Survey Photographic Collection, Library of Congress
National Archives and Records Administration
National Association of CCC Alumni
Tutwiler Collection of Southern History and Literature, Birmingham Public Library
U.S. Forest Service, Montgomery, Alabama
UAB Archives, University of Alabama at Birmingham
University of Alabama Museums, Tuscaloosa, Alabama
Walter B. Jones Photograph Collection, Alabama Museum of Natural History, The University of Alabama Museums

PREFACE

As the U.S. stock market plummeted in late 2007, this book was envisioned as a visual survey of the first federal stimulus program and how it was expended in the Birmingham area during the 1930s.

Carolanne Roberts chose the title and the lead photograph for our project: workers digging earth for dirt-cheap houses being built at Mount Olive. Thomas Hibben Jr., an innovative federal architect and engineer, was supervising the adaptation of an ancient building technique known as rammed earth for use in low-cost housing in this federally sponsored farming community, now a suburb north of Birmingham. Hibben photographed his experimental construction techniques and the inexpensively built houses.

Hibben's photograph is part of a remarkable collection of 164,000 remaining Depression-era negatives made by Resettlement Administration (later the Farm Security Administration) photographers hired by innovative Washington bureaucrats to document the benefits of federal expenditures. To the Birmingham area, the Washington staffers sent some of the nation's finest photographers—Walker Evans, Carl Mydans, Arthur Rothstein, and Marion Post Wolcott—with specific shoot lists to document federal housing programs here. In Birmingham, from 1935 to 1939, these individuals photographed working and living conditions at area industrial mines and mills and documented the houses and well-designed suburban communities that the government was financing and building in rural areas near the city. The Farm Security Administration–Office of War Information Photographic Collection is today housed at the Library of Congress and online (*http://memory.loc.gov/ammem/fsahtml/fahome.html*).

The records of the Historic American Buildings Survey (HABS), which began in 1933 with unemployed architects making measured drawings and photographs of pre-1860 structures, continue to this day as an archive of drawings, photographs, and other materials documenting America's architectural heritage. These materials, which document more than 38,600 historic structures, can be found at the Library of Congress, where they are a frequently used and online collection (*http://memory.loc.gov/ammem/collections/habs_haer*).

The Birmingham Public Library, especially its Southern History and Archives Departments, also holds significant visual resources from the New Deal period. Throughout the years, the library's dedicated staff have safeguarded source material, including the engineer's copy of Jefferson County's heavily illustrated final report documenting the work of the Civil Works Administration (CWA); the James M. "Jimmie" Jones Papers (Jones was President of the Birmingham City Commission at this time); manuals to implement the federal programs (including the school lunch room program); the tax assessor files on county property, first formulated through on-site property inspections in 1938 by Works Progress Administration (WPA) workers; teaching aides; and art work accumulated as libraries expanded their missions and collections during the 1930s. Don Veasey, Curator of Photographs, was invaluable in locating obscure records in the Archives collections, and Yolanda Valentin and Gigi Gowdy did yeoman work providing digital reproductions. Also of invaluable assistance were the clipping files found in the Southern History Department. Here, since the 1930s, librarians have gathered newspaper and print sources on many pertinent topics. The library also holds a microfilm copy of the Jefferson County WPA projects card file, the transcription of which provided descriptions of local WPA projects, noting recipients—cities, counties, and federal, state, and local agencies—the required match, the total project cost, and the number of persons employed.

Renee Blaylock, Director of the Birmingham Public Library, asked department heads to help locate pertinent Depression-era records in their collections. She also directed Elizabeth Swift, Integrated

Library Systems Administrator for the Jefferson County Library Cooperative, to establish a Web site to showcase the library's New Deal resources. Swift created *The New Deal in Jefferson County*, an online exhibit that accompanied the first phase of this project, which was the Birmingham Historical Society's photographic exhibit *Digging Out of the Great Depression–Federal Programs at Work* (November–December 2009). Library staff continue to add to the Web site (*http://www.bplonline.org/resources/exhibits/new_deal*) as more information becomes available.

Robert Pasquill Jr., a Montgomery-based U.S. Forest Service archaeologist and dedicated chronicler of the work of the Civilian Conservation Corps (CCC) in Alabama, lent his expertise and access to photographic resources of the U.S. Forest Service and his personal collection. His good friend and Society Trustee Brian Rushing photographed extant CCC structures in Alabama's state parks. Bob's book, *The Civilian Conservation Corps in Alabama, 1933–1942: A Great and Lasting Good* (Tuscaloosa: University of Alabama Press, 2008), provides further details about the men and work of the Alabama CCC.

Birmingham-Southern College Assistant Professor Pam Venz and her students—Adam Colbert, Charles Horn, Annette Kittrell, Jamie Neal, Andrew Ryan, and Booth Wilson—helped us research 1930s structures in Birmingham parks during a 2003 Jan-term photographic studio. Peggy Balch contributed significant research to this effort. Many of the projects, we discovered, were funded through a City of Birmingham bond issue of 1931, prior to the expenditure of federal funds. Concerned about idled industrial workers, civic leaders such as James R. McWane led the campaign to build recreational facilities in the parks.

The University of Alabama Museums provided yet another treasure trove of visuals and information, made readily accessible by the online WPA/TVA Archaeological Photographs (*http://diglib.lib.utk.edu/wpa*). This extensive archive contains photographs taken by WPA workers of archaeological projects conducted in preparation for Tennessee Valley Authority (TVA) dam construction in the 1930s. Mary Bade and Mike Dressler provided access to these records, and archaeologist Eugene Futato kindly reviewed our brief summary of archaeological work at this time.

At the Birmingham Botanical Gardens Library Archives and Rare Book Room, Archivist Jason Kirby cleaned up the storage area and, to the delight of all, unearthed the personal scrapbooks of the state's WPA beautification program supervisor. These materials chronicle the many efforts of the federal program administrator, together with scores of community groups, to "beautify" roads, schools, and other public places.

Frank Jefferson Tombrello and Graham C. Boettcher, the latter the William Cary Hulsey Curator of American Art at the Birmingham Museum of Art, greatly expanded our knowledge of federally supported art remaining in public and private collections, especially those of the Birmingham Museum of Art (*http://www.artsbma.org*), the Montgomery Museum of Fine Arts (*http://www.mmfa.org*), Patrick Cather, and Jane, Harold, and Hubert Goings. Tombrello photographed many pieces for this book, including the spectacular school and post office murals. Alice Carter at the Montgomery Museum helped research federally funded traveling exhibits shown at the Montgomery Museum in the 1930s.

Sallie Lee, then a Jefferson County Agent of the Alabama Cooperative Extension System, or ACES (*http://www.aces.edu*), as well as a Society Trustee, brought to our attention the *Historical Panorama of Alabama Agriculture*, the fabulous canvas mural panels recently rediscovered in the attic of the ACES office on the Auburn University campus. ACES Art Specialist C. Bruce Dupree's research documented the work as that of a Mobile WPA artist who created the series for the 1939 Alabama State Fair in Birmingham. The panels showcased New Deal pride in technological and agricultural progress that was helping to build a better life for Alabama's farmers. Through the efforts of Gaines Smith, ACES Director, and Carol Whatley, Communications and Marketing Director, ownership of the murals has been transferred to the Jule Collins Smith Museum of Fine Art in Auburn (*http://jcsm.auburn.edu*). Museum Director Marilyn Laufer is supervising the cleaning and restoring of the murals for their return to

Birmingham for a showing at the Birmingham Historical Society–Birmingham Public Library exhibition *Murals, Murals On the Wall, 1929-1939–Our Story Through Public Art*, appearing in the Library Gallery from November 7 to December 31, 2010.

Major portions of this book, through the financial support of the Daniel Foundation of Alabama and the Alabama Humanities Foundation, a state program of the National Endowment for the Humanities, first appeared as an exhibit at the Birmingham Public Library. *Digging Out of the Great Depression–Federal Programs at Work* exhibited in the Library Gallery from November 1 to December 31, 2009.

We hope you agree that the book provides superb visual demonstration of federal programs at work and evidence of many people working.

Field Crew Seated on the Domiciliary Mound, Bessemer Site 15 Je 14.
Photograph, August 30, 1939. Courtesy The University of Alabama Museums, Tuscaloosa, Alabama.

Introduction

"Hard times come here first and stay longest." That's how those in Birmingham speak of the Great Depression. President Franklin D. Roosevelt called the city "the worst hit town in the country."

As the 1930s opened, Birmingham was the center of an industrial region with mines and mills and the manufacture of iron and pipe at the core of its idled economic engine. When Roosevelt took office in March 1933, 25 percent of the national labor force was without jobs. In Birmingham, widespread unemployment had been high for some time.

In 1930, 68 percent of those employed in the city worked in blast furnaces, steel mills, foundries, and fabricating plants. Jefferson County's industrial wage earners numbered 76,662. Most of these workers saw their wages and hours cut drastically as employers attempted to weather the downturn. Thousands of others were without jobs.

The city's steel production sank to its lowest 1930s level in 1932. The steel mills never closed, but production averaged 40 percent to 60 percent of capacity. Blast furnaces and ore mines operated only sporadically. Coal mining fared a bit better.

In July of 1934, one-fourth of the population of Birmingham and Jefferson County was listed as receiving federal aid. Of 56,000 families on relief state-wide that December, 28,000 lived in Birmingham. Only World War II, with its heavy demand for structural steel and armament, provided the stimulus required to revive the district's industrial economy.

This book explores federal programs designed to cut the relief rolls and ameliorate the lives of residents of the greater Birmingham area during the 1930s. Diverse programs implemented here employed more than 24,000 persons and expended more than $1 billion in today's dollars.

Alabama's politicians and citizens were committed to bringing federal dollars to our community. At their opening meeting in the winter of 1933, the bankers, clergy, and businessmen who headed up the local Civil Works Administration (CWA) committee noted their desire to secure "every possible dollar" they could. The photographs from their final reports demonstrate what they accomplished, in just five months, with a federal infusion valued at $39.3 million in today's dollars. They felt and responded to the community need.

Succeeding federal programs carried the relief efforts forward.

The Works Progress Administration (WPA), the nation's largest employer in this era, put more than 9,000 persons to work in Jefferson County. WPA workers improved infrastructure: roads, bridges, hospitals, schools, and parks. They improved drainage and airport runways. They built health and TB clinics and public buildings. They sealed abandoned coal mines. They greatly expanded recreational facilities at schools and at state and local parks, playgrounds, and athletic fields. They staffed libraries and parks to keep them open extra hours to provide recreational opportunities. They operated sewing rooms to make clothing and house wares for needy families. They staffed the first school lunch room programs. They painted history murals for public schoolchildren and for state fairgoers. They drew scenes of everyday life and taught art and music in the schools. They wrote and staged theatrical productions. They transcribed city and county records. They photographed and recorded property for the tax assessor's office. They recorded graves in area cemeteries. They painted schoolhouses and planted roses. One thousand strong, they excavated archaeological sites across the state. They worked.

The Public Works Administration (PWA), a bricks-and-mortar arm of the Department of the Interior, provided partial funding for the Industrial Waterworks System through the creation of Inland Lake (an expenditure that included WPA labor estimated at a $94 million value in today's funds). Jefferson

Tower at today's UAB Medical Center (a $34.5 million dollar project in today's funds) was built as a hospital for needy persons—the project in which local politicians took the greatest pride. In 1938, Smithfield Court became the first Birmingham public housing project, followed by Elyton Village in 1940. Both projects were built with PWA funds in conjunction with the local public housing authority, which was established at this time. By April 1943, additional housing projects at Central City, Eastwood, and Southtown provided Birmingham 2,566 total public housing units valued at $213 million in today's dollars, representing the largest federal expenditure in the area.

The Civilian Conservation Corps (CCC)—"Roosevelt's Tree Army"—worked at nearby Oak Mountain State Park and at Cheaha State Park on reforestation, road and building construction, fire suppression, erosion control, and other projects. They also built today's Moundville Archeological Park and Jones Archaeological Museum near Tuscaloosa.

At a total cost of $53.3 million dollars in today's funds, the Resettlement Administration (RA) built four new communities at Greenwood, Mount Olive, Palmerdale, and Trussville. With the National Park Service, the RA also built a Recreational Demonstration Area at Oak Mountain State Park surrounding today's Tranquility Lake. RA photographers, including Walker Evans, Thomas Hibben Jr., Carl Mydans, Arthur Rothstein, and Marion Post Wolcott, provided a superb record of federal initiatives here to improve housing alternatives and lifestyles for industrial workers.

The federal relief efforts of the 1930s touched the lives of virtually every resident of Birmingham and Jefferson County. The beneficiaries of these programs—the men and women who labored to improve their lot and that of the community—left us with a remarkable legacy.

What major New Deal landmarks remain?

- Bessemer City Hall
- Chalkville State School for Girls
- Fairfield Post Office and City Hall
- Roads, bridges, drainage improvements, fish hatchery, lodge, picnic shelters, and an arboretum at Lane Park—now Birmingham Zoo
- Greenwood, Mount Olive, Palmerdale, and Cahaba Village at Trussville communities
- *Historical Panorama of Alabama Agriculture*, Auburn
- Industrial Waterworks System, now part of the Birmingham Water Works system
- McAdory High School
- Moundville Archeological Park, Tuscaloosa
- Murals at East Lake Branch Library, Fairfield Post Office, Lakeview School (now Martin Advertising Building), Montevallo Post Office, and Woodlawn High School
- Nine stadia and grandstands in Jefferson County, including H. F. Gilmore–Melvin Vines Stadium in Hueytown and Snitz Snider Memorial Stadium in Bessemer
- Oak Mountain and Cheaha State Park improvements
- Overton Park, Homewood
- Rosedale School, Homewood
- Scores of additions to Birmingham and Jefferson County schools, especially auditorium, class- and lunchroom wings, and recreational amenities
- Slossfield Negro Youth Training Center, North Birmingham
- Smithfield, Elyton, and Southtown housing projects
- Stone structures in local and state parks
- Tuberculosis Sanatorium, now Lakeshore Foundation
- Vulcan Monument and Park

WELCOME ADDRESS BY HON. J. M. JONES, JR., PRESIDENT, CITY COMMISSION, TO MRS. ELEANOR ROOSEVELT AT 8 O'CLOCK, P.M., MARCH 23, 1937, AT MUNICIPAL AUDITORIUM.

Mr. Chairman, Ladies and Gentlemen, and Our Most Distinguished Guest:

It is impossible for me to adequately express the hearty welcome which all of our people feel toward the First Lady of the Land. The whole American people gave some idea of this feeling when the Roosevelt Administration was again placed in charge of our national government by the greatest landslide in our history. My friends, the feeling which we have in our hearts tonight is more than a feeling of welcome; it is a feeling of deep appreciation, pride and honor that Mrs. Eleanor Roosevelt has come to our city.

In 1933, the people of Birmingham were honored by a visit from our illustrious President. Only one thing marred the happiness of that occasion; his distinguished wife did not accompany him. But tonight, she has also done honor to our city, and we are now satisfied and contented.

Since March 1933, the White House has come to mean more to the American people than ever before. During the late depression no city suffered more than industrial Birmingham. Our banks were failing; our industries were closing; our people were without employment; we were without a market for our municipal bonds; we were unable to take care of our thousands of people on relief. In our dire distress the Roosevelt Administration came to our rescue. It restored confidence. It placed the country's banking system on a sound basis; it bought Birmingham's bonds; it enabled us to complete our drainage system; it supplied funds for the construction of much needed viaducts, underpasses, and many miles of pavement and various other public improvements. It spent two million dollars in our city for slum clearance, and it is furnishing six and one-half million dollars for the construction of our great and much needed industrial water system. It has furnished employment for thousands of our citizens. It has fed our needy and clothed our naked.

My friends, the outlook for the city of Birmingham was never brighter. With the timely help of the Roosevelt Administration and with the progressive spirit of our people, the depression has been conquered. Birmingham has the same inexhaustible resources she has always had, the same mountains rich in coal and ore, the same rivers, the same fertile valleys. The sun shines even more brightly than it has in the past. Birmingham now the great metropolis of Alabama, is destined soon to become a city of a million people, and the metropolis of our entire Southland.

But, my friends, our guest of tonight is distinguished not only because she is the wife of one of the greatest presidents of all history, she is distinguished because of her own ability and attainments. Mrs. Roosevelt, we have followed your career with profound interest. We know that it is from you that our great leader draws his support and inspiration. Happy is the nation which has a wise and able leader to whom it may look for inspiration; blessed, indeed, is the nation which has two such outstanding leaders.

And now permit me figuratively, at least, to present to you the keys to our city. These keys will unlock for you our picturesque driveways from which you may look down in the valley upon Birmingham, a scintillating gem at the feet of the mountains so full of coal, iron and limestone. These keys will unlock the doors of our great industrial plants which the Roosevelt Administration has again set in motion, and from which go out manufactured steel and iron products to the utmost parts of the world. They will unlock our places of amusement, our shows and theatres, our clubs, our parks and libraries. They will unlock to you our homes. They are, indeed, the keys to our hearts. This is a great day in the history of our City. It is a memorable day for the people of Alabama. Mrs. Roosevelt, Birmingham's door of welcome was never swung wider open than it is to you tonight.

I thank you for your attention.

Welcome Address by James M. Jones Jr., City Commission President, to Eleanor Roosevelt, March 23, 1937, Municipal Auditorium.
James M. "Jimmie" Jones Papers, File #1007. Department of Archives and Manuscripts, Birmingham Public Library (BPL Archives).

Cartoon Parody of Roosevelt's New Deal Program.
Vaughn Shoemaker.
Courtesy The Franklin D. Roosevelt Presidential Library and Museum, administered by the National Archives and Records Administration.

Roosevelt holds a hand of alphabet cards, which he is organizing on the table like a game of Scrabble.

Chapter One
Alphabet Agencies

Beginning in 1932, Acts of Congress and Presidential Executive Orders established so many new agencies that they became known by their initials. In 1936, a peacetime year, federal spending first outpaced that of state and local governments. It rose to nine percent of the national economy.

January 1932–1941, **Reconstruction Finance Corporation (RFC)** lent $9.4 billion in low-interest loans to banks, insurance companies, building and loan associations, agricultural credit organizations, and railroads to help stabilize these institutions.

March 1933, **Emergency Banking Act (EBA)** closed and helped reorganize troubled banks.

April 1933–1942, **Civilian Conservation Corps (CCC)** established a work relief program for more than 3 million men from unemployed families who planted trees, built roads and structures, and fought fires in the nation's forests and parks. *The CCC's closest projects to Birmingham were at Oak Mountain and Cheaha State Parks and at today's Moundville Archaeological Park near Tuscaloosa.*

May 1933–December 1935, **Federal Emergency Relief Administration (FERA)** operated a direct-relief effort that provided jobs for more than 20 million people and granted $3.1 billion to local work projects.

May 1933–present, **Tennessee Valley Authority (TVA)** became the first large federal regional planning agency. TVA built dams, produced and sold hydroelectric power and fertilizer, developed recreational lands and communities, and reforested this region.

May 1933–1937, **Agricultural Adjustment Act (AAA)** began the federal balancing of supply and demand for farm crops by offering farmers funds to not produce corn, cotton, milk, peanuts, rice, tobacco, and wheat.

June 1933, **National Industrial Recovery Act (NIRA)** authorized the President to regulate industry and permit cartels and monopolies. The act also guaranteed labor the right to organize and bargain collectively. *An amendment sponsored by Alabama Senator John Bankhead Jr. created the Subsistence Homestead program.*

June 1933–1943, **Public Works Administration (PWA)** spent $4 billion on federal, state, and local construction projects, funding educational buildings, courthouses, public art, sewage-disposal plants, waterworks and public health facilities, and streets and roads. *The major Birmingham projects were the Industrial Waterworks System at Inland Lake; the Jefferson Hospital, now part of UAB; and public housing projects, the first at Smithfield and Elyton.*

June 1933, **National Recovery Administration (NRA)** allowed industries to create "codes of fair competition," which were intended to reduce "destructive competition" and to help workers by setting minimum wages and maximum weekly hours. Blue Eagle posters symbolized business participation in the NRA.

June 1933–present, **Federal Deposit Insurance Corporation (FDIC)** guaranteed the safety of bank deposits up to a certain amount.

June 1933–1936, **Home Owners' Loan Corporation (HOLC)** permanently changed the prevailing mortgage system, refinancing more than a million homes to prevent foreclosure.

1933–present, **Farm Credit Administration (FCA)**, established in 1916, was authorized to establish a centralized source of farm credit.

September 1933–present, **Soil Erosion Service (SES)**, now the Natural Resources Conservation Service of the United States Department of Agriculture, was established to assist farmers.

October 1933–1939, and to present, **Commodity Credit Corporation (CCC)** aided farmers and producers through loans, purchases, and other operations. In 1939, the CCC was transferred to the United States Department of Agriculture.

October 1933–March, 1934, **Civil Works Administration (CWA)**, a five-month program, employed 4 million people in the construction of roads, schools, playgrounds, airports, and sewers. The program spent over a billion dollars nationally. *The CWA employed 15,000 persons in Jefferson County in public works projects.*

October 1933–March 1934, **Public Works of Art Project (PWAP)** commissioned more than 15,000 works of art for public buildings. A Treasury Department program continued the work through 1943.

1933–present, **Historic American Buildings Survey (HABS)** began a make-work program for unemployed architects to develop measured drawings of pre-1860 architecture and thereby develop a national architectural archive that remains to this day. *HABS documented the Walker, Worthington, and Mudd Plantation houses in Birmingham.*

1934, 1938–present, **Bureau of Air Commerce, Civil Aeronautics Authority–Federal Aviation Authority (CAA–FAA)** expanded the federal role in air travel, monitoring safety, overseeing pilot and aircraft certifications, and regulating fares and routes.

June 1934–present, **Federal Communications Commission (FCC)** became the successor to the Federal Radio Commission, regulating non-federal broadcasting and interstate and international telecommunications that originate in the United States.

1934–present, National Housing Act of 1934 created the **Federal Housing Administration (FHA)** and the Federal Savings and Loan Insurance Corporation to improve housing standards and conditions and provide home financing by insuring mortgage loans. The FHA is today part of the **Department of Housing and Urban Development (HUD)**. *From 1934 to 1938, Robert Jemison Jr. of Birmingham was the FHA's first state director for Alabama.*

1934–present, **Securities and Exchange Commission (SEC)** was charged with protecting the interest of the public and investors in connection with the public issuance and sale of corporate securities.

October 1934–June 1943, U.S. Treasury Department's **Section of Fine Arts** encompassed variously named programs that commissioned works of art for post offices and courthouses across the nation and for public buildings in Washington, D.C. *The best-known local projects are the post office murals at Fairfield and Montevallo.*

1934, July 1935–present, **National Labor Relations Board (NLRB)**, the successor organization to the National Labor Board of 1933, conducted elections for labor union representatives and investigated and remedied unfair labor practices.

April 1935–1943, **Works Progress Association-Administration (WPA)**, name changed to Works Project Administration in 1939, employed more than 8.5 million persons in communities across the nation to work on 19 types of potentially fundable activities, including improving streets, roads, and schools and building highways, bridges, airports, water systems, and parks. *The WPA employed 9,000 persons in Jefferson County on public works projects valued at $637 million in today's dollars. A partial list of local projects follows in Chapter Five.*

April 1935–present, **Resettlement Administration (RA)**, later **Farm Security Administration (FSA)**, now **Farmers Home Administration** attempted to improve the lifestyle of sharecroppers, tenant farmers, and the rural poor by resettling them on large government-owned farms that used modern techniques and expert supervisors. *One activity set up 34 subsistence homestead communities under the guidance of government experts, four of them in the Birmingham area at Greenwood, Mount Olive, Palmerdale, and Trussville. Federal photographers documented these community building efforts.*

May 1935–1942, **Federal Art Project (FAP)** was an "art for every man" program and sub-unit of the WPA that hired artists from the relief rolls to produce and exhibit more than 400,000 works of art, provide art education for children, and staff 100 community art centers.

June 1935–1943, **National Youth Administration (NYA)**, a part of the WPA, provided vocational educational programs for adult learners and work to keep other students in school. Aubrey Williams from Alabama headed the program. *The NYA was active at the Slossfield Clinic in North Birmingham and the Snow Rodgers and other community centers. NYA and WPA workers also built Overton Park in Homewood.*

July 1935–1939, **Federal Writers' Project (FWP)** funded writers of local and oral histories, children's books, and the 48 state guide books known as the American Guide Series. FWP workers also indexed titles, including the *Index to Alabama Biography,* slave tales, life histories, short stories, and folklore. Individual states continued the project until 1943.

August 1935–present, **Social Security Board–Administration** became law and remains so, with social security benefits financed by a payroll tax.

1935–1943, **Federal Music Project–Program** gave employment to professional musicians and teachers of music. The program hosted thousands of concerts and festivals, offered music lessons, created 34 orchestras, and researched American traditional music and folk songs.

1935–1939, **Federal Theatre Project** funded theatrical events: classical and children's venues, revues, musical comedies, vaudeville, circus, dance, puppet and marionette shows, and ethnic plays. Coordinated from Washington, its theatre companies operated in 22 states and 40 cities, including Birmingham, which became home to the only federally supported African-American theater unit in the Deep South.

May 1935–1955, **Puerto Rico Reconstruction Administration (PRRA)** intended to provide agricultural relief and economic diversification as well as power, good roads, reforestation, and adequate housing.

May 1935–present, **Rural Electrification Administration (REA)** undertook to provide farms with inexpensive electric lighting and power. The Rural Utilities Service continues this function today.

1930s and 1940s, **Recreational Demonstration Area (RDA)** program was a National Park Service program that built and staffed 46 public parks in 24 states, chiefly near urban areas. *Oak Mountain State Park included an original Recreational Demonstration Area with a group camp in the area about Tranquility Lake that was created at this time.*

1937, **United States Housing Authority (USHA)** was designed to lend funds to states or communities for the low-cost construction of public housing. The Housing Act of 1937 provided for the establishment, through state law, of local public housing authorities to build, own, and operate housing and for the government to guarantee mortgages for other low-cost housing developments. *In 1938, Smithfield Court became the first Birmingham project and was followed by Elyton Village in 1940. These were built with PWA funds. By April 1943, additional housing projects at Central City, Southtown, and Eastwood provided Birmingham 2,566 total public housing units, valued at $213 million in today's dollars.*

June 1938, **Fair Labor Standards Act** established a minimum wage and a maximum work week.

Chapter Two
Putting the First 15,000 to Work:
The Civil Works Administration (CWA)

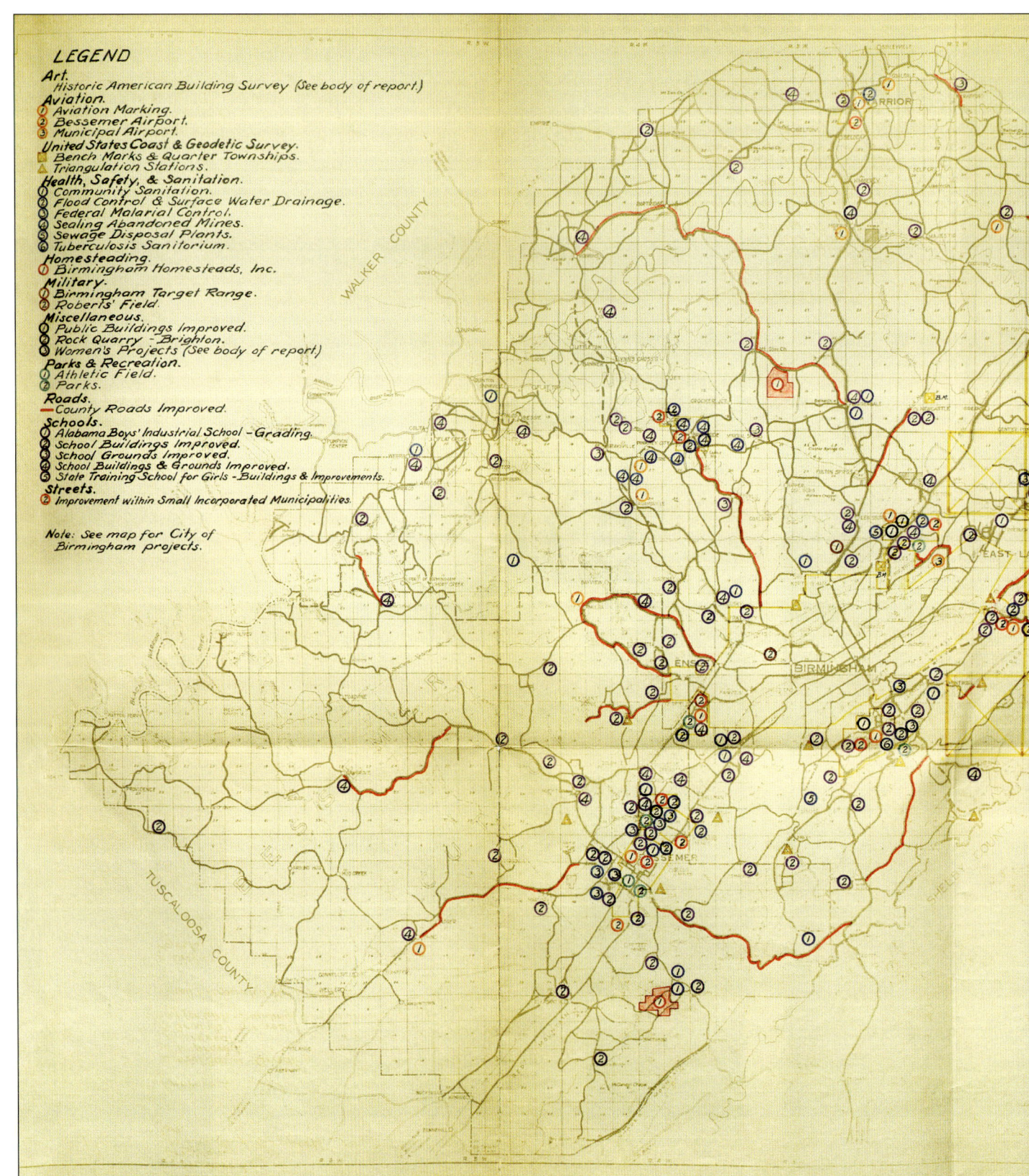

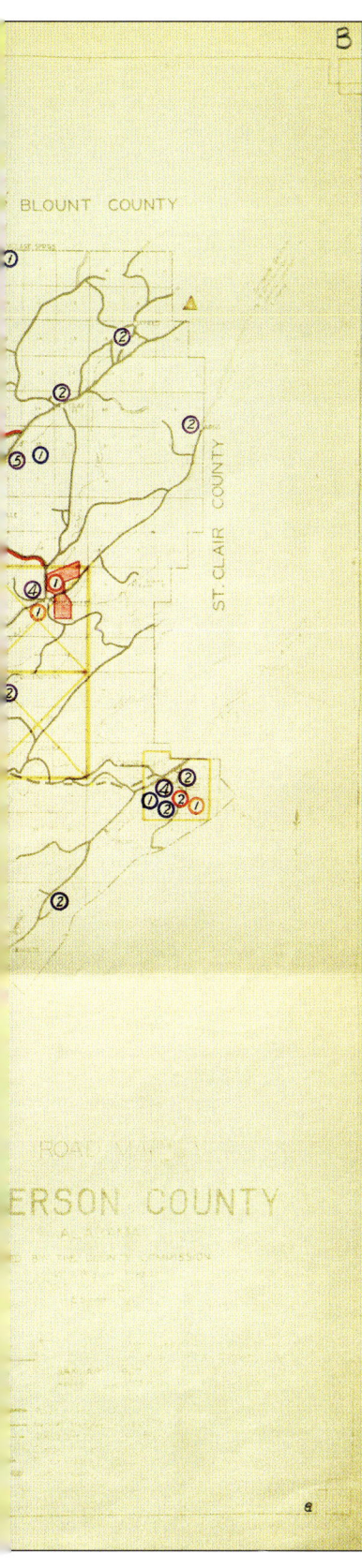

The first federal program established to create temporary jobs for millions of unemployed citizens was unveiled November 8, 1933. Nationally, it provided jobs for 4 million persons and spent more than $200 million a month, well above initial cost estimates. The program ended on March 31, 1934.

The program was managed in Jefferson County under the direction of a local committee that included a leading clergyman, two bank presidents, a lawyer, an investment banker, an industrialist, and a housewife. They met on November 20, 1933, the day after the local initiative was announced, and declared their purpose to "put every possible man to work at the earliest possible date, with the idea of securing every possible dollar for the residents of Jefferson County." Their track record is admirable.

By the end of the first week, 5,816 persons from all types and classes of work were employed on projects countywide. By February 15, 1934, 15,350 persons were employed. The program expended $3.6 million in federal dollars and the required $250,000 local match. It would have completed all its projects had federal authorities not curtailed the work week to 24 hours per week to reduce run-away expenditures.

The county engineer's copy of the *Report of the Civil Works Administration of Alabama, Jefferson County Division*, now held in the Southern History Department of the Birmingham Public Library, documents with words and photographs the remarkable improvements made in the five-month period to public facilities, streets and roads, storm water drainage, parks, and schools and athletic fields in the Birmingham area. A partial list includes:

- 92 miles of roads improved
- Streets, alleys, sidewalks, and storm drains improved
- Additions made to the airport and other public buildings
- 101 county schools repaired, renovated, and cleaned
- New park facilities and school athletic fields built
- 74 playground leaders assigned to supervise play in parks
- Repairs made to 11 buildings at the TB Sanatorium
- 500 coal mine openings sealed to decrease acidity in the surface water carrying mine drainage
- 400 boxes of donated toys given to the Community Christmas Shop and placed in new kindergarten programs started in the parks
- 12 reading rooms opened to extend library services (These had "trained directrices.")
- 13 persons hired to keep the libraries open on the weekends
- 15 sewing rooms organized with 140 seamstresses who produced 13,371 garments
- 24 nurses hired to advance public health initiatives
- 2 women appointed to inventory and index state and county records

Map of Jefferson County Project Sites.
Published in Report of the Civil Works Administration of Alabama, Jefferson County Division, *1934. Courtesy Birmingham Public Library (BPL) Southern History Department.*

The map documenting the City of Birmingham projects, cited on the county map, *left*, is missing from the library's volume.

Public Facility Improvements

Shades Valley Sewage Disposal Plant, Jefferson County.
"A general view of the Shades Valley Disposal Plant showing the clarifier tanks, flocculators and main building. Also digestor tanks in the background. This is one of the most modern sewage treatment plants using the chemical process in the U.S."
Published in Report of the Civil Works Administration of Alabama, Jefferson County Division, *1934*.
Courtesy BPL Southern History.

Municipal Garage, Tarrant.
"This is one of several projects of Tarrant City where skilled men were used to advantage on public buildings."
Published in Report of the Civil Works Administration of Alabama, Jefferson County Division, *1934*.
Courtesy BPL Southern History.

City Shops, Birmingham.
"A general view showing the construction of the new City Shops located at the South Side Jail property. The material used in the construction of this building was salvaged from the Loveman Joseph & Loeb Fire."
Published in Report of the Civil Works Administration of Alabama, Jefferson County Division, *1934*.
Courtesy BPL Southern History.

STREET AND ROAD IMPROVEMENTS

Repairing Streets—Brick Paving, Bessemer.
"Repairing the worn out brick paving on 19th Street, Bessemer. This paving has been in a bad condition for a number of years. The bricks are taken up and turned over and reset on sand cushion and grouted, and all worn out bricks are replaced with new bricks."
Published in Report of the Civil Works Administration of Alabama, Jefferson County Division, *1934*.
Courtesy BPL Southern History.

Grading and Surfacing a Residential Street, 33rd Avenue from 16th to 17th Street, North Birmingham.
"A typical section of one of the many streets graded and surfaced in the North Birmingham district of the City of Birmingham."
Published in Report of the Civil Works Administration of Alabama, Jefferson County Division, *1934*.
Courtesy BPL Southern History.

Grading and Surfacing, 25th Avenue from 22nd to 24th Street, North Birmingham.
"A typical street grading and surfacing job in the negro section of North Birmingham."
Published in Report of the Civil Works Administration of Alabama, Jefferson County Division, *1934*.
Courtesy BPL Southern History.

Broadway Cut, North View, Homewood.
"This road is a continuation of the present paved street in Homewood known as Broadway that follows the car line to the paved road along Edgewood Lake. This road was cut through solid rock and will give the people of this section a more direct route into Homewood and Birmingham."
Published in Report of the Civil Works Administration of Alabama, Jefferson County Division, *1934*.
Courtesy BPL Southern History.

Rocky Ridge Road, Elimination of Dangerous Curve, Jefferson County.
"This view of the Rocky Ridge Road clearly shows the extent of road work in Jefferson County. New right of ways were secured in order to make this major change to eliminate some of the dangerous curves of this road."
Published in Report of the Civil Works Administration of Alabama, Jefferson County Division, *1934*.
Courtesy BPL Southern History.

Grading, 83rd Street South of Vassar Avenue, Birmingham.
"A typical view of a street grading job in the South part of East Lake."
Published in Report of the Civil Works Administration of Alabama, Jefferson County Division, *1934*.
Courtesy BPL Southern History.

Widening and Straightening, Maxine Road, Jefferson County.
"This view shows another change being made in the Maxine Road that winds through the mountains near the Warrior River. This singular change will eliminate three dangerous horse shoe curves. This was the heaviest road project in Jefferson County."
Published in Report of the Civil Works Administration of Alabama, Jefferson County Division, *1934*.
Courtesy BPL Southern History.

Grading and Widening, East Lake Boulevard, Tarrant.
"East Lake Boulevard is the main street through Tarrant City connecting the county road from East Lake to the business section of this city and the paved Mt. Pinson Road. This road was formerly a narrow curving road through cuts and fills and has been widened to its full width and made safe for the travelling public."
Published in Report of the Civil Works Administration of Alabama, Jefferson County Division, *1934*.
Courtesy BPL Southern History.

Widening and Straightening, Bradford–Mt. Pinson Road, Jefferson County.
"This is one of the heavy travelled roads in this section of the county, leading into several mining camps and on into Warrior, Alabama. Curves have been day-lighted through heavy rock cuts, and this road has been reworked for a distance of approximately 5 miles."
Published in Report of the Civil Works Administration of Alabama, Jefferson County Division, *1934*.
Courtesy BPL Southern History.

Storm Water Improvements

Streets, Sidewalks, and Drains, Central Park, Birmingham.
"An end view of a 3' x 11'3" stone box storm sewer with reinforced cone slab. This box culvert is 900' long and replaces an open ditch that ran through a beautiful park and across several streets in Central Park."
Published in Report of the Civil Works Administration of Alabama, Jefferson County Division, *1934*.
Courtesy BPL Southern History.

Drainage Ditch and Concrete Bridge, Interurban Heights, Fairfield.
"This view is of the [main] ditch showing the end of one of the many concrete bridges built along this ditch through this colored village."
Published in Report of the Civil Works Administration of Alabama, Jefferson County Division, *1934*.
Courtesy BPL Southern History.

Parking Field and Treatment of Gutter, Municipal Airport, Birmingham.
"A typical section of the parking space along the east side of the Municipal Airport showing area graded and surfaced with course slag. The gutter between this parking area and the County Road has been lined with large flat stone 6' wide to allow for drainage and easy cross-over for cars."
Published in Report of the Civil Works Administration of Alabama, Jefferson County Division, *1934*.
Courtesy BPL Southern History.

Drainage Ditch, Municipal Airport, Birmingham.
"Typical section of drain ditch showing treatment of side walls of ditch with ruble masonry."
Published in Report of the Civil Works Administration of Alabama, Jefferson County Division, *1934*.
Courtesy BPL Southern History.

Streets, Sidewalks, and Drains, Lomb Boulevard, Birmingham.
"A picture of one of the concrete box storm sewers showing a section of the open ditch. This sewer eliminates several wooden bridges in Lomb Boulevard in the vicinity of the Fair Grounds in the City of Birmingham."
Published in Report of the Civil Works Administration of Alabama, Jefferson County Division, *1934*.
Courtesy BPL Southern History.

Drainage Ditch, Green Springs Park—Now George Ward Park, Birmingham.
"A view of a typical section showing treatment of drainage ditches with rip-rap-ruble masonry in Green Springs Park."
Published in Report of the Civil Works Administration of Alabama, Jefferson County Division, *1934*.
Courtesy BPL Southern History.

Park Improvements

Recreation Building, Homewood Park, Homewood.
"One of the units of the new Homewood Park on Shades Creek." [Status: Demolished for Brookwood Mall.]
Published in Report of the Civil Works Administration of Alabama, Jefferson County Division, *1934*.
Courtesy BPL Southern History.

Community House, Municipal–Now Roosevelt Park, Bessemer.
"The Community House is one of the many units of the Municipal Park constructed by the C.W.A. This house is of a permanent construction and equipped with a large open room and fire place, a nursery, kitchen, two toilets and lavatories." [Status: Under restoration by the Bessemer Parks Department.]
Published in Report of the Civil Works Administration of Alabama, Jefferson County Division, *1934*.
Courtesy BPL Southern History.

Wading Pool and Spring House, Municipal Park–Now Roosevelt Park, Bessemer.
"Two other units of the Municipal Park at Bessemer, showing the wading pool and spring house. This spring is the main source of water supply for wading pool and swimming pool." [Status: Filled in.]
Published in Report of the Civil Works Administration of Alabama, Jefferson County Division, *1934*.
Courtesy BPL Southern History.

Barbecue Pit, Lane Park, Birmingham.
"A picture of one of the barbecue pits built in Lane Park of rustic stone masonry. These pits and shelter houses are built throughout this park to serve individual picnic groups. The park covers an area of 200 acres." [Status: Extant at the Birmingham Zoo.]
Published in Report of the Civil Works Administration of Alabama, Jefferson County Division, *1934.*
Courtesy BPL Southern History.

Stone Bridge, Lane Park, Birmingham.
"One of the rustic bridges built with stone quarried from Lane Park. This bridge is built over a spring branch on one of the drives through this park." [Status: Extant on Pullen Creek, just east of the train station at the Birmingham Zoo.]
Published in Report of the Civil Works Administration of Alabama, Jefferson County Division, *1934.*
Courtesy BPL Southern History.

Community House, Lane Park–Now Zoo Lodge, Birmingham.
"A view of the beautiful Community House in Lane Park. This house is built from natural stone taken from this park and equipped with modern plumbing and other features." [Status: Renovated by the Birmingham Zoo in 1992–1993 and rented for special events.]
Published in Report of the Civil Works Administration of Alabama, Jefferson County Division, *1934.*
Courtesy BPL Southern History.

Athletic Fields and Other School Improvements

Athletic Field, Ensley High School, Birmingham.
"A view of the Ensley High School athletic field showing the leveling and sprigging of these grounds."
Published in Report of the Civil Works Administration of Alabama, Jefferson County Division, *1934*.
Courtesy BPL Southern History.

Athletic Field, Hueytown School, Jefferson County.
"This is another County School that was built years ago on a site where it was necessary to do a large amount of grading in order to build a suitable playing field adjacent to the school building. This work was all done with hand labor."
Published in Report of the Civil Works Administration of Alabama, Jefferson County Division, *1934*.
Courtesy BPL Southern History.

Athletic Field, Tarrant City School, Tarrant.
"The work of grading this athletic field together with the landscaping and drainage of these grounds represents one of the best completed projects of the C.W.A."
Published in Report of the Civil Works Administration of Alabama, Jefferson County Division, *1934*.
Courtesy BPL Southern History.

Athletic Field and Terrace, Lewisburg School, Jefferson County.
"A view showing the treatment of terraces and slopes of the deep cut showing the stone steps and retaining wall. The stone used in the construction of this wall was taken from nearby abandoned coke ovens."
Published in Report of the Civil Works Administration of Alabama, Jefferson County Division, *1934*.
Courtesy BPL Southern History.

Football Field and Stand, Bessemer.
"This view shows the arrangement of this field and the type of construction of the grandstand."
Published in Report of the Civil Works Administration of Alabama, Jefferson County Division, *1934*.
Courtesy BPL Southern History.

Matrons Home, State Training School for Girls, Chalkville.
"This was one of the old buildings which has been remodeled and made into a 6-room house for the Matrons Home. This is one of the several units of this project."
Published in Report of the Civil Works Administration of Alabama, Jefferson County Division, *1934*.
Courtesy BPL Southern History.

Painting, Mortimer Jordan High School, Jefferson County.
"This picture shows the painting of the Mortimer Jordan High School, a typical painting project. Similar work of this kind has been done throughout Jefferson County."
Published in Report of the Civil Works Administration of Alabama, Jefferson County Division, *1934*.
Courtesy BPL Southern History.

Addition, Springdale School, Jefferson County.
"This new building replaces an old dilapidated building that was being used as an annex to this school."
Published in Report of the Civil Works Administration of Alabama, Jefferson County Division, *1934*.
Courtesy BPL Southern History.

Auditorium, Warrior High School, Jefferson County.
"An interior view of the new auditorium of Jefferson County High School at Warrior, Alabama."
Published in Report of the Civil Works Administration of Alabama, Jefferson County Division, *1934*.
Courtesy BPL Southern History.

Chapter Three
Roosevelt's Tree Army
The Civilian Conservation Corps (CCC)

In March 1933, President Franklin Roosevelt created the Civilian Conservation Corps (CCC) to put men to work on natural resource projects. Alabama took full advantage of this popular program.

Lands were reforested and protected from erosion and fire, timber productivity was developed in the newly acquired national forests and on private land, and recreational facilities were built at many state parks. Between 1933 and 1942, an average of 30 CCC camps operated in Alabama. The state's total participation was $55 million.

The Moulton Advertiser of July 16, 1942, provides a statistical summary of the work of Alabama's CCC boys:

- 1,800 miles of roads built
- 490 bridges constructed
- 188 buildings erected for the protection and administration of forest lands and for public recreational areas
- 1,430 miles of telephone lines strung
- 61 lookout towers built
- More than 2,200 miles of firebreaks constructed
- More than 285,000 bushels of pine cones gathered
- 20,000 denuded areas replanted to provide future forests
- 114,000 acres of timber improved
- Numerous recreational areas developed with improved hunting and fishing

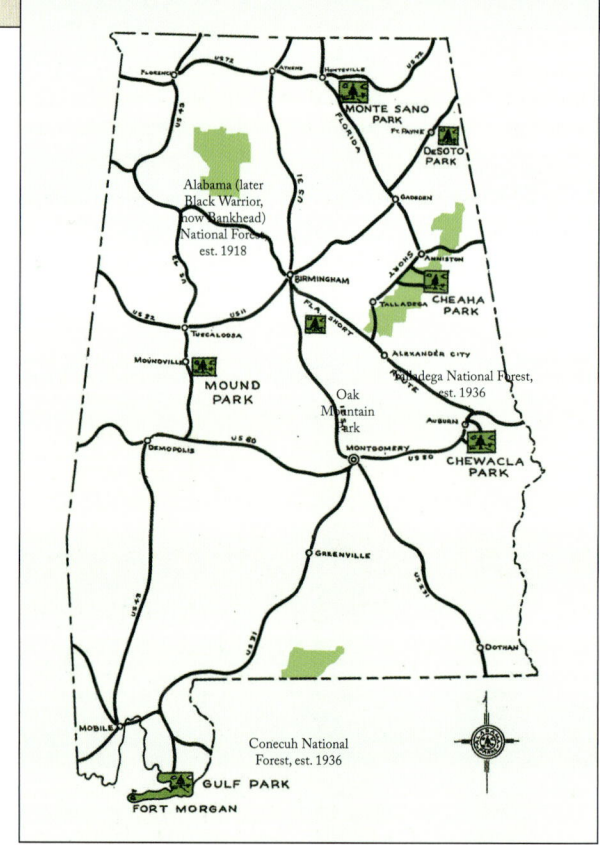

Map of Alabama National Forests and State Parks in CCC Days, 1933–1942.
Adapted from State Parks in Alabama, *a brochure by the State of Alabama, Parks Division, Department of Conservation, Montgomery, Alabama, 1940.*

Company Photograph, 1935. Company 3475, Camp F-2 at Danville, Alabama (now Bankhead) National Forest.
Photograph courtesy Robert Pasquill Jr.

CCC enrollees were organized into companies of approximately 200 men each. Large-format photographs of assembled companies were made as souvenir portraits and sold to the men. Recruits were assigned to a camp and usually served for three months. The closest camps to Birmingham were SP-8 and P-81 at Bessemer.

Sentell Martin, 1937. Company 3477-C, Camp F-6 at Heflin, Talladega National Forest.
Photograph courtesy Robert Pasquill Jr.

Company leaders organized the men for their project work and camp life. Leaders were paid $45 monthly, well above the $30 monthly base pay. Enrollees sent home to their families a portion of this pay. Sentell Martin was a company leader and also edited the company newspaper and played the piano.

Telephone Line Crew with Supervisor, 1937. Company 3477-C, Camp F-6 at Heflin, Talladega National Forest.
Photograph courtesy Robert Pasquill Jr.

Men were assigned various duties, including the rigging of telephone lines between fire towers to assist in fire protection. Aided by the "climbers" on their legs, this crew climbed trees to string the lines.

THE MEN AND CAMP LIFE

Camp P-54 for Company 2403 at Brewton, 1933.
Photographs courtesy the National Association of CCC Alumni and Robert Pasquill Jr.

In the beginning, enrollees were housed in tents provided by the army. Each man was issued army clothing and two blankets. Toiletries and mess kits were also supplied.

Soon camps grew to average 24 buildings, including a kitchen and mess hall, recreation and education buildings, infirmary, barracks accommodating as many as 40 to 50 men, and quarters for the military and technical staff.

**Charles Foster, CCC Artist, 1934.
Company 463, Camp F-1 at Moulton,
Alabama (now Bankhead) National Forest.**
Photograph courtesy Robert Pasquill Jr.

Under a program created by First Lady Eleanor Roosevelt, artists recorded CCC camp life. Foster spent four months photographing and preparing watercolor and oil paintings of Alabama's first CCC camp, established May 19, 1933, in the future Bankhead National Forest.

**Barracks for Company 463, 1934.
Camp F-1 at Moulton, Alabama–
(now Bankhead) National Forest.
Watercolor by Charles Foster.**
Photograph courtesy Robert Pasquill Jr.

Mess Hall, 1933.
Camp P-54 at Brewton.
Photograph courtesy the National Association of CCC Alumni and Robert Pasquill Jr.

Enrollees of Company 3486, 1936.
Camp TVA P-13 at Huntsville.
Photograph courtesy the National Association of CCC Alumni and Robert Pasquill Jr.

In this souvenir photograph, *below*, CCC men are gathered in the Education Building, where reading and writing as well as vocational education instruction was offered.

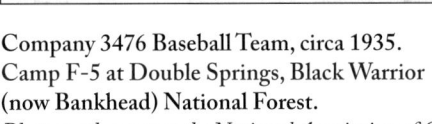

Company 3476 Baseball Team, circa 1935.
Camp F-5 at Double Springs, Black Warrior (now Bankhead) National Forest.
Photograph courtesy the National Association of CCC Alumni and Robert Pasquill Jr.

Most CCC camps organized sporting teams. Opponents included other camp and high school teams. In isolated areas, barracks played other barracks and work crews took on other crews. Singing groups, movies, drama, and dances were also popular.

Work Crew Heading Out of Camp, 1936.
Company 3478-C, Camp F-7 at Chandler Springs, Talladega National Forest.
Photograph courtesy U.S. Forest Service.

Work in the Forests

Constructing a Fire Tower, Talladega National Forest, circa 1936.
Photograph courtesy U.S. Forest Service.

The Talladega National Forest was acquired in 1936. *At left*, enrollees in Company 3477-C construct one of nine steel fire towers the CCC built in the newly acquired forest. These towers reduced the time needed to report and take action on forest fires.

Fire Tower at Open Pond, Conecuh National Forest, 1938.
Photograph courtesy U.S. Forest Service.

This 100-foot steel fire tower with a 12- x 12-foot "cab" and an exterior catwalk is one of four such towers built by CCC men in Conecuh National Forest, which was also created in 1936.

Caretaker's Cabin, Weogufka State Park, 1935.
Photograph courtesy U.S. Forest Service.

A watchman lived in this residence adjacent the fire tower on Flagg Mountain. Mississippi farm boys and native Alabamians built it as well as Weogufka's roads, towers, cabins, bathhouse, and mess hall. From 1933 to 1935, Company 260 lived at the park while building its structures from timber and stone hewn on-site.

Bunker Tower at the Highest Spot in Alabama, Cheaha State Park, Built 1934–1935.
Photograph by Robert Pasquill Jr., 2007.

Men from Alabama, Florida, and Georgia who formed Company 468 built a 13-mile road from their camp at Oxford into the wilderness area that was to become Cheaha State Park. Then, they began work on this 40-foot tower, as well as cabins and other structures. Those who worked on the stone bridges, culverts, and retaining walls along the park road learned on the job. Their leader was the only man experienced in masonry when construction of the park road began.

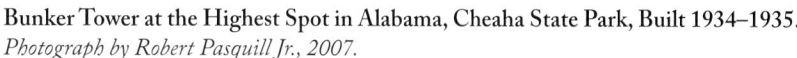

ROOSEVELT'S TREE ARMY

Fire Suppression and Forest Regeneration

Filling Back-Pack Pumpers, Talladega National Forest, 1936.
Photograph courtesy U.S. Forest Service.

Enrollees patrolled the forests with fire-fighting equipment. In 1935, a Talladega newspaper reported that two CCC companies in the adjacent national forest had extinguished 700 forest fires. *At the left*, enrollees from Company 3478-C at Camp F-7 at Chandler Springs fill their pumpers.

Fire Suppression in the Talladega National Forest, 1936.
Photographs courtesy U.S. Forest Service.

Enrollees on the Cheaha State Park project from Company 468 at Camp SP-7 also helped fight fires in Alabama's national forests.

Collecting Pine Cones, Blue Pond Plantation, Conecuh National Forest, 1937.
Enrollees from Company 3474-C at Camp F-9 near Andalusia.
Photograph courtesy U.S. Forest Service.

When Conecuh National Forest was created in July 1936, it consisted of 54,177 acres of cutover and burned-over lands. The land was mostly barren except for scattered trees that logging operators had considered undesirable. CCC enrollees collected seeds and planted seedlings to help reforest the Conecuh lands.

Planting Pine Seedlings, Blue Pond Plantation, Conecuh National Forest, 1937.
Photographs courtesy U.S. Forest Service.

Blue Pond became the Alabama CCC's first large-scale planting project. In January 1937, 60 enrollees planted 22,000 trees in one day. Six weeks later, nearly a million trees had been planted on 1,000 acres here. To regularly space the pine seedlings at 6- by 8-foot intervals across the open lands, the planting crew "followed the knotted string." Both longleaf and slash pine were planted.

Timber Stand Improvement, Talladega National Forest, 1937.
Photograph courtesy U.S. Forest Service.

To help the newly planted pine grow, CCC men cut down damaged trees and tree species that competed with the pines. Here, the work is performed by Company 3478-C of Camp F-7 at Chandler Springs.

Erosion Control, Open Pond, Conecuh National Forest, 1937.
Photograph courtesy U.S. Forest Service.

To stop erosion on over-timbered and over-farmed land, the Alabama CCC built hundreds of check dams similar to those pictured. In this photograph, the forest supervisor and district ranger inspect the dams. Above the dams, *top of this photograph*, CCC Camp F-9 is perched at the top of the gully.

Building Roads and Bridges

Five Runs Creek Bridge, Conecuh National Forest, 1937.
Photographs courtesy U.S. Forest Service.

Enrollees of Company 3474-C at Open Pond built this bridge, *below*, and planted its approaches with "carpet grass sod," *left*.

Thompson Creek Bridge, Alabama (now Bankhead) National Forest, 1933.
Photograph courtesy U.S. Forest Service.

Enrollees of Company 1403 at Kinlock Springs built this steel-span bridge with masonry abutments.

Bridge Construction Crew from Company 1485, Camp S-52 at Chunchula.
Photograph courtesy National Association of CCC Alumni and Robert Pasquill Jr.

ROOSEVELT'S TREE ARMY

BUILDING RECREATIONAL AREAS AND A MUSEUM

OPEN POND RECREATIONAL AREA

Drilling a Well, Open Pond, Near Andalusia, 1937.
Photograph courtesy U.S. Forest Service.

Before building the recreational area, the CCC men drilled a well to provide water for drinking, bathing, and lavatory facilities.

Open Pond Recreational Area, Conecuh National Forest, 1938.
Photograph courtesy U.S. Forest Service.

The recreational area for bathing and picnicking included a bathhouse, picnic shelter, tables, and barbecue pits all built by Company 3474-C of Camp F-9. The 200 enrollees also built roads, constructed fences, and planted trees over the 3,000-acre area. When the recreation area opened in June 1938, the *Covington News* noted that the bathhouse, *center left in the photograph below,* "built of large hewn timbers, in its setting among the majestic pines portrays a beautiful and restful atmosphere to the surroundings."

THE MUSEUM AT MOUNDVILLE

Pouring the First Concrete for the Museum at Mound State Monument, May 24, 1937. *Photograph made by Dr. Walter B. Jones, Courtesy the Walter B. Jones Photograph Collection, Alabama Museum of Natural History, University of Alabama Museums.*

This major archaeological site was purchased in 1932 by the State of Alabama. CCC men constructed its first roads and trails, initiated erosion control to stabilize the 26 mounds, and built a concrete museum building. Archaeologists Dr. Walter Jones and Dr. James DeJarnette and others also supervised CCC enrollees in the excavation of the mounds. At this time, the age and contents of the mounds were unknown.

To work at the Moundville site, CCC Company 487 established a side camp from their main camp SP-8 at Bessemer. Later, Company 444 established a full camp at the park, Camp SP-15. They completed the museum to house the site's archaeological collection for its opening on May 16, 1939. Robert Flechner, Director of the CCC, was on hand to help celebrate. Today the mounds, artifacts, and museum remain at the Moundville Archaeological Park.

Construction of the Mound State Monument Museum, Moundville, 1939.
Photograph courtesy the Walter B. Jones Photograph Collection, Alabama Museum of Natural History, University of Alabama Museums.

Cheaha State Park

"Sky Way Motor Way" Construction, Talladega National Forest, 1937.
Photograph courtesy U.S. Forest Service.

The Talladega National Forest was created in July 1936. Several CCC companies were assigned to make the forest more accessible. Company 3477-C from Heflin constructed the scenic road, which extended from Sylacauga to Borden Springs across the more than 2,000 acres of Cheaha State Park and the highest point in Alabama: a location 2,407 feet above sea level.

Bankhead Fire Tower and Picnic Shelter, Talladega National Forest, 1938.
Photographs courtesy U.S. Forest Service.

During 1936, 17 miles of the Talladega scenic road were located, graded, and cherted. By March 1937, 180 CCC men were working to develop the emerging Cheaha State Park. They constructed the fire tower, *above*, and a watchman's house, *far right*, as well as visitor amenities including picnic shelters, overnight cabins, and a bathhouse—all of native timber and stone hewn on the site. CCC work continued here in 1938 and 1939.

Lunchtime for Construction Crew, "Sky Way Motor Way" Project, Talladega National Forest, 1937.
Photograph courtesy U.S. Forest Service.

Mess hall workers provided lunch, which was served from the back of a truck to CCC men who consumed it at the job site with utensils from their army-surplus mess kits.

Watchman's House, Talladega National Forest, 1938.
Photograph courtesy U.S. Forest Service.

In the photograph, *right*, the National Forest District Ranger reviews construction plans for the watchman's dwelling with the CCC Project Superintendent. A carpenter works to the rear.

Watchman's House Above the Sky Way Motor Way, Talladega National Forest, 1938.
Photograph courtesy U.S. Forest Service.

Cheaha State Park and the scenic drive reopened to visitors in June 1939. Park improvements included visitor accommodations, 30 miles of road, and 4 miles of foot trails. Four thousand native shrubs and trees had been transplanted to the park area.

State Parks in Alabama

State Parks in Alabama

GULF
CHEWACLA
CHEAHA
DeSOTO
MONTE SANO
MOUND

THE Candid Camera FINDS in Alabama's State Parks Many Thrilling and Interesting Subjects

From the crest of Cheaha Mountain, 2,400 feet above sea level, to Gulf Park, on the southernmost shores of Baldwin County overlooking the Gulf of Mexico, one may find every type of scenery, climate and recreation. Waterfalls, gorges, forests, mountains, white sandy beaches, picturesque lakes, rivers —all in varying degrees of splendor and majesty—are here to entice the outdoor lovers.

Instead of operating the entire system of 14 parks in a hap-hazard manner, the State Parks Division of the Conservation Department selected a few of the most attractive parks for development at this time, and has concentrated all its resources in making these chosen few complete in every respect both as to equipment and recreational advantages. Gulf Park, Chewacla, Cheaha, DeSoto and Monte Sano are the five first-class resorts fully equipped this year, while Mound State Monument, although without overnight cabin accommodations, is complete in every other respect. Little River, near Atmore in South Alabama, and Oak Mountain, near Birmingham, each have overnight cabins and are open to the public at this time.

Alabama's park properties were constructed by the Civilian Conservation Corps under direction of the National Park Service, and the investment represents millions of dollars. Unlike the thickly populated states in other sections of the country, Alabama's outdoors offers unlimited opportunities to enjoy Nature in solitude and quietness if one so desires.

FOR INFORMATION AND RESERVATIONS
Write
Parks Division, Department of Conservation
Montgomery, Alabama

Vacation Cabin Rentals

Park	Address of Custodian	Cabins	Per Night, Fri. Sat. and Sun.	Per Night, Mon. Tue. Wed. Thurs.	Per Week (7 days)	No. of Persons
Monte Sano	Huntsville	11 Cabins	each $3.00	$2.00	$15.00	4
Cheaha	R. 2 Munford	7 Cabins	each 3.00	2.00	15.00	4
Chewacla	Auburn	2 Cabins	each 3.00	2.00	15.00	4
		2 Cabins	each 4.00	3.00	20.00	6
DeSoto	R. 1 Ft. Payne	14 Cabins	each 3.00	2.00	15.00	4
			each 3.50	2.50	17.50	5
			each 4.00	3.00	20.00	6
Gulf	Foley	4 Upland Cabins	each 1.75	1.50	9.00	4
		5 Lakeside Cabins	each 2.50	2.00	12.00	4
		2 Lakeside Cabins	each 4.00	3.00	18.00	8
		2 Duplex Apartments	each 3.25	2.75	15.00	6
		Entire Duplex to one party	each 6.00	4.70	25.00	12
Little River	R. 2, Atmore	3 Cabins	each 1.75	1.25	9.00	4
Oak Mountain	R. 1, Helena	6 Cabins	each 2.50	1.75	12.00	4
			each 3.00	2.25	15.00	5
			each 3.50	2.75	18.00	6

Cabin Equipment

Cabins are completely furnished and all you need to bring is ice. Kerosene for cooking can be obtained from the park custodian at all parks except Monte Sano, where electric hot plates are furnished. Cabin furnishings include beds and cots, complete with bedding; towels; cooking utensils; dishes and cutlery; chest of drawers; table and chairs; stove with oven for baking; ice box or refrigerator. Kerosene lamps are used for lighting at Cheaha and Oak Mountain.

Reservations

Cabin reservations should be booked for three or four weeks in advance if possible, by writing the Custodian, giving number of persons in party, date and hour reservation is to begin, length of stay, etc. The reservation cannot be completed until a deposit is made. If the cabins are not available for the time specified, all money will be returned to the applicant. For additional information write Parks Division, Department of Conservation, Montgomery, Alabama.

ALABAMA invites you to enjoy A Vacation in her State Parks . . .

If you like to fish, there are miles and miles of running streams and acres of fresh water lakes. Boats are available at nearly all the parks and you can fish to your heart's content.

If you prefer hiking, there are miles of excellent trails winding over the hillsides, through cool forests and beside clear streams.

To those who simply want to rest and relax, a quiet cabin in one of the State parks is the ideal place.

In any case, the time will not hang heavy on your hands, for there is something to do at all times.

The Parks Division of the Department of Conservation has spared no effort to complete the equipment and recreational facilities of the parks. Governor Frank M. Dixon is heartily in sympathy with the park work and it is his wish to provide the people of this and other states with the very best in outdoor recreational advantages.

A custodian is in charge of each park and his instructions are to leave nothing undone to assure the vacationist a pleasant and enjoyable outing.

Again, Alabama invites you to enjoy a vacation in her State parks. If you come once, you surely will return.

Boating on a lovely stream in Chewacla State Park.

Air view of Mound State Monument

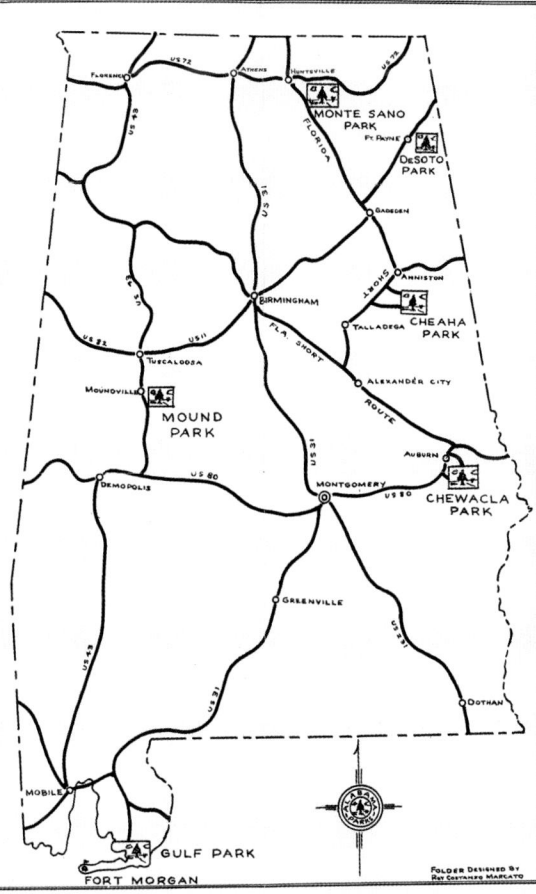

Rhododendron in DeSoto Park is an appropriate frame for the face of this pretty miss.

MONTE SANO STATE PARK Approximately four miles from Huntsville, this mountainous park has 2,110 acres with 15 miles of picturesque hiking trails and 10 miles of splendid bridle paths. There are 11 roomy stone cabins (see rates on another page of this folder); a lodge where meetings, dances and other social gatherings may be held; and a lounge for cabin occupants. A complete waterworks system furnishes clear sparkling water. Picnicking facilities include tables, benches, ovens, fireplaces, barbecue pits and shelters. Electricity is used for lighting and other purposes. A dining room will serve meals at nominal cost and a stable is maintained where riders may obtain mounts. A concessionaire's stand furnishes soft drinks. The mountain scenery in Monte Sano is unexcelled, including a cavern known as Natural Well. Leading from the city of Huntsville to the park is a parkway. The highest point in Monte Sano is 1,600 feet above sea level.

DESOTO STATE PARK The gorgeous rhododendron framing the girl at the right, as well as wild azaleas, are to be found on the hillsides of DeSoto State Park during the Spring. To see the flowers is an experience never to be forgotten. DeSoto, in the mountain region of DeKalb and Cherokee Counties near Fort Payne and Mentone, comprises 4,649 acres characterized by its great length and unusual variety of scenic and recreational possibilities. There are 14 cabins, two of them being duplex style. A dining room serves meals to the vacationists. Picnicking facilities, such as fireplaces, shelters, barbecue pits and tables, are available. A golf course has been built through co-operation of local groups and is open. There are many interesting side trips to points of historical interest from DeSoto. Beautiful DeSoto Falls is nearby and there is good fishing in streams of the park. Volley ball and horse shoe pitching may be enjoyed. May's Gulf, resembling the Colorado Grand Canyon on a reduced scale, is unique to the eastern United States.

MOUND STATE MONUMENT The burials seen above are the remains of a prehistoric people whose civilization flourished in Alabama long before the arrival of the first white man on this continent. Commonly called the Mound-Builders, they were the first Americans. Descendants of a race of people which originated in Central Asia and migrated to America by way of the Bering Straits, this group settled on the banks of the Black Warrior River near the present town of Moundville. Here they built their village of crude wooden structures with the huge mounds of earth constructed for bases on which their temples were placed; the highest mound is 58-1/2 feet high, the broadest covers 1¾ acres. Thirty-four known mounds are in the three hundred acre tract which is being developed by the CCC and the National Park Service in cooperation with the Alabama Museum of Natural History. A permanent Museum housing two in-situ burial pits and artifacts from the area is now open to the public. Overnight facilities are not contemplated but picnicking is provided for. At Moundville you have the opportunity of viewing one of the world's premier archaeological sites.

This stone cabin, completely furnished inside is typical of those in Alabama State parks.

CHEAHA STATE PARK The stone observation tower shown on the cover of this folder rises from the crest of Cheaha Mountain, 2,400 feet above sea level and the highest point in the State of Alabama. This park comprises 2,638 acres in the counties of Clay, Talladega and Cleburne. It is a few miles south of Anniston. Seven new cabins, picnic facilities and plenty of places to fish and swim are to be found at Cheaha. The water reservoir near the top of the mountain is the highest impounded body of water in the State. At the west base of the mountain a lake has been impounded for bathing purposes and there is a large stone bath house at the edge of the lake. Preservation of the natural and primitive, rather than its obliteration has been the aim of the parks authorities, and there are large areas reserved for hiking. Without a doubt, Cheaha offers a magnificence in mountain scenery unrivalled in the South.

A 26-acre lake impounded above a picturesque waterfall provides bathing for vacationists at Chewacla State Park.

CHEWACLA STATE PARK The bathers in the picture above are enjoying the splendid recreational advantages of Chewacla State Park, comprising 525 acres in Lee County, Alabama. There is a lake of 26 acres impounded above a picturesque waterfall where swimming and fishing may be enjoyed. Part of the park lies in the so-called fall line separating the plateau or Piedmont region from the coastal plain. Five stone cabins are available for the public and there is a new bath house with accommodations for about 800 people. Picnic facilities include shelters, tables, fireplaces, etc. There is a playfield for soft ball and volley ball, as well as horse shoe pitching. Hiking over the numerous trails affords pleasure and recreation. Chewacla is near one of Alabama's institutions of higher learning—Alabama Polytechnic Institute at Auburn—and this gives the area a special value in recreational and cultural life.

Air view of historic Fort Morgan, Gulf State Park. (Below)

GULF STATE PARK Accepted as one of the outstanding resorts on the entire Gulf coast, this park's facilities are in heavy demand from the public. It has 4,522 acres; a mile of excellent beach on the Gulf of Mexico; three fresh water lakes; a varied semi-tropical flora; a parkway 22 miles long extending to historic Fort Morgan on the western tip of the long peninsula that juts out to protect Mobile Bay; and many other recreational features. There are 16 cabins, including one duplex (see rate list). The beautiful casino building, standing on the dunes only 700 feet from the Gulf and about 1,000 feet from one of the fresh-water lakes, cost several thousand dollars. It houses bathing accommodations for 2,000 people; a restaurant overlooking the beach; and sun porch. The large central hall is suitable for dances and other entertainments. Swimming is under the supervision of accredited lifeguards. Boats may be rented for fishing in the freshwater lakes which is excellent. Salt water fishing guides also may be obtained near the park. Gulf Park's beach has been pronounced one of the best on the entire Atlantic or Gulf coasts, with its pure fine white sand and blue water. Fort Morgan, one of the most important historical sites in Alabama, is only 22 miles away by paved road and there one may explore underground dungeons and passages of the ancient fortress, examine the 14-inch disappearing guns, and walk with the dead past of 200 years ago.

This stone bathhouse at Cheaha State Park is typical of buildings at other units in the State park system

State Parks in Alabama.
Brochure by the State of Alabama, Parks Division, Department of Conservation, Montgomery, Alabama, 1940.

This brochure presents Alabama's state parks, and their recently built recreational amenities, to future park visitors. It also suggests that, "Alabama's outdoors offer unlimited opportunities to enjoy Nature in solitude and quietness if one so desires." The new CCC-built museum at today's Moundville Archaeological Park is also included in the presentation.

A Great and Lasting Good: CCC Structures in Alabama's Parks

Alabama's state parks contain a wealth of well-built Civilian Conservation Corps construction work. Designated in 1927, the state parks developed facilities for visitors during the 1930s using improvements from the Adirondack resort tradition, then the popular model for the national parks and forests. This basic park scheme included hiking, picnicking, camping (in cabins and tents), and swimming. The parks became woodland retreats with rustic facilities built of rough-cut stone and crude timber hewn on-site.

Brian Rushing's 2009 photographs for Birmingham Historical Society record typical CCC features: scenic roads to the highest and most scenic point in the park, bridges, observation towers, dams (to create lakes), ridge-top and lakeside cabins for overnight visitors, bathhouses for swimmers, group lodges, picnic shelters, and barbecue pits, all created and set into the woods with great respect for the natural and indigenous landscape.

Oak Mountain State Park

In late 1934, CCC men from their camp near Bessemer began developing the first 940 acres of this 9,940 acre park. They graded and surfaced the Pea Vine Falls Road to the highest point in the park, where lookout points offer views for miles. Birmingham engineer Henry Gladner, Jemison & Company's engineer for the development of Mountain Brook Estates, supervised the construction of this road and the Red Road. Oak Mountain Park, with CCC-built picnic facilities, staff houses, and trails, opened in 1936.

From 1935 to 1942, the Resettlement Administration, together with the National Park Service, developed the Group Camp at Tranquility Lake on additional park acreage now extensively used by the Boy Scouts.

Pea Vine Falls Road

Bridge, Pea Vine Falls Road

Picnic Shelter

Bridge, Pea Vine Falls Road

Cheaha State Park

In 1936 and 1937, CCC men built the scenic "motorway" into the park, accessing the highest point in Alabama. Here, they located Bunker Tower. At that point, the observation tower originally also included park administration and a gift shop. The tower, bluff-side cabins, and a group lodge have welcomed visitors since the park opened in June 1939.

Bunker Tower

Bunker Tower

Bald Rock Lodge

Overnight Cabins Along the Bluff

ROOSEVELT'S TREE ARMY

Park Orientation Building

Mound State Monument – Now Moundville Archaeological Park

CCC labor built roads and facilities and also helped archaeologists Walter Jones and James DeJarnette and others excavate portions of the Mississippian-era (A.D. 1000 to A.D. 1450) village's many mounds at this 320-acre site overlooking the Black Warrior River. The museum and other facilities reopened in 2010, following the major renovation seen in these 2009 photographs. Moundville has been nominated to become a UNESCO World Heritage site. The park, under the aegis of the Alabama Museum of Natural History, first opened in 1939.

Park Orientation Building

Today's Jones Archaeological Museum

Chewacla State Park

At this 525-acre park in Lee County near Auburn, the CCC built a dam that created a lake for swimming and fishing. CCC labor also built the immense stone bathhouse, said to accommodate 800 people, and five cabins to provide accommodations for overnight park visitors. An Auburn-based advocacy group currently seeks to preserve the character of the scenic road leading into the park.

Dam Impounding the 26-Acre Chewacla Lake

Park Office

Cabin by the Lake

Bath House

Picnic House

Bath House

ROOSEVELT'S TREE ARMY 37

CHAPTER FOUR
BETTER HOUSING FOR INDUSTRIAL WORKERS:
SUBSISTENCE HOMESTEADS AND PUBLIC HOUSING

The first New Deal housing initiative was incorporated into the National Industrial Recovery Act of 1933. An amendment sponsored by Alabama Senator John Bankhead Jr. created the Homesteads Division of the Department of the Interior (later part of the Resettlement Administration, the Farm Security Administration, and the Federal Public Housing Authority).

The homesteads program, established in July 1933, set out to build farming communities for wage earners of modest means to help them supplement their uncertain industrial income. Nationally, this experiment in government-financed, cooperative farming drew controversy. In the South, part-time farming to enhance income was a way of life. Most families in small towns and rural communities made a garden and kept chickens, a milk cow, and perhaps hogs. Because this was not possible in urban areas, the program, targeted for rural areas near Birmingham, found favor here, particularly with the slack in operation of mines, mills, and furnaces.

In Birmingham, a local committee, headed by industrialist Erskine Ramsay, selected the four tracts of land deemed suitable for subdivision into small farms. The sites were located less than 20 miles from Birmingham, to which the part-time farmers would carpool to jobs in the city and at industrial sites.

In 1935, the Resettlement Administration, the Washington agency that managed the building of the homesteads, set up a construction office in Birmingham to supervise projects in Alabama, Florida, Georgia, Mississippi, and South Carolina. The office employed 180 men. As many as 2,500 local men were hired from relief rolls and paid good wages to build the Birmingham projects. Local landscape professionals laid out the Birmingham communities, and local architects designed most of the houses as well as a combined school and community center and a cooperative store at each location. Most construction materials for homesteads were purchased from Birmingham suppliers. A plethora of government inspectors ensured the best workmanship. Agricultural experts provided farming know-how. The four communities were up and running by April 1938, five years after the initial legislation.

By 1944, when the subsistence homesteads program closed, the federal government had built 34 new homestead communities consisting of 3,304 homes at a cost of $30 million. Through this and various other federal housing programs, a total of 99 new communities with 10,938 new units were built at a cost of $108 million. Among the 99 communities were Cahaba Village–Trussville, Greenwood, Mount Olive, and Palmerdale near Birmingham, as well as Bankhead Farms in Walker County, Skyline Farms in Jackson County, Gee's Bend Farms in Wilcox County, and Prairie Farms in Macon County, the latter two projects for African Americans.

"Roadside Stand near Birmingham, Alabama."
Photograph by Walker Evans, 1936.
Courtesy the Library of Congress Farm Security Administration-Office of War Information Photograph Collection (LOC-FSA).

BETTER HOUSING FOR INDUSTRIAL WORKERS

Documenting Working and Living Conditions

The Resettlement Administration (later the Farm Security Administration) hired photographers to gather documentation showing how the New Deal's social reforms might improve people's lives. This photographic work, which was published in local newspapers and popular magazines of the era, is most responsible for creating the visual image of the destitution wrought by the Great Depression.

The Birmingham photographs—made by Walker Evans, Carl Mydans, Thomas Hibben Jr., Arthur Rothstein, and Marion Post Wolcott from 1935 to 1939—do not show destitution. They capture workers and their families, mines and mills, and company quarters adjacent to these industries. Several of the families from the local sites photographed would be among those selected to move into the new communities at Greenwood, Mount Olive, Palmerdale, and Trussville that Resettlement Administration professionals were designing and building at this time.

In the photographs, the mines and mills are functioning, albeit on a part-time basis. The varied housing stock pictured in the photographs dates from the 1880s to the mid–1920s. Since the founding of Birmingham in 1871, industrial firms had built and rented quarters for their employees at the work site, this often being the only place to live in the then undeveloped region. The surrounding landscapes are often barren and stripped of valuable minerals. For the photographs that follow, the photographers' original captions, cited with quotation marks, remain as the title of each photograph.

"Steelmill and workers' houses. Birmingham, Alabama."
Photograph by Walker Evans, 1936.
Courtesy the Library of Congress Farm Security Administration-Office of War Information Photograph Collection (LOC-FSA).

This photograph shows the iron-producing furnaces at TCI-U.S. Steel's Ensley Works, not steel mills as the image's original caption states. A steam engine hauling ladle cars filled with molten iron, *center*, heads to the steel mill, *to the left and not pictured in the photograph*. At this mill, the molten iron was further processed into steel and steel rail, then the principal product of the Ensley Works. Double shotgun houses for furnace labor appear in the foreground.

"Steel plant and workers' houses. Birmingham, Alabama."
Photograph by Marion Post Wolcott, May 1939.
Courtesy LOC-FSA.

This photograph, made from a vantage point further west than the Walker Evans image on the previous page, also shows the company quarters at the Ensley Works. It is wash day. The houses photographed are bungalow-style duplexes built for the company's expanded labor force of the 1920s. Each worker and his family are provided three rooms and electricity. Front porches have then-stylish brick piers supporting the porch columns.

"Steelmill workers' company houses and outhouses. Republic Steel Company, Birmingham, Alabama."
Photograph by Walker Evans, March 1936.
Courtesy LOC-FSA.

Republic Steel did not make steel in Birmingham. At its Thomas site, it manufactured iron as well as coke and coke byproducts, the coolers for which plant are pictured here, *far left,* with adjacent company houses and outhouses.

Local industrial firms built these one-story houses by the hundreds in the early 1900s. Known as "square tops," the cottages are well adapted to the Southern climate. Hot air rises into the steep roof, effectively cooling the rooms below. With two front doors, the house was easily subdivided as the demand for housing changed. The company provided electricity, but sanitary facilities were outside. Several of the square top houses remain today in the Thomas neighborhood of the city of Birmingham.

"An iron ore mine near Bessemer, Alabama. Some of the Rehabilitation [Resettlement] Administration homesteaders work here."
Photograph by Arthur Rothstein, February 1937.
Courtesy LOC-FSA.

This photograph shows the above-ground mining facilities at TCI-U.S. Steel's Muscoda Red Ore Mine No. 4, including the tipple, hoist house, machine shop, and Mineral Railroad spurs. Red Mountain has been heavily stripped of its surface ore. That ore was transported via the Mineral Railroad, *bottom*, to the company's ironmaking furnaces just five miles away at Ensley and Fairfield. Many of the mining facilities and the adjacent miners' housing remain today, just west of Red Mountain Park.

"Iron ore miners. Jefferson County, Alabama."
Photograph by Arthur Rothstein, 1937.
Courtesy LOC-FSA.

Birmingham area miners and the nearness of the ore mines to the furnaces made possible the cheap iron for which the region was noted. In 1922, the price per ton of Alabama red ore was $1.54; the average U.S. price was $3.14.

"Iron ore mine and company houses. Jefferson County, Alabama."
Photograph by Arthur Rothstein, April 1937.
Courtesy LOC-FSA.

This view from the mining operations on Red Mountain (note the cars filled with ore, *at the bottom left of the photograph*) looks across the valley in which rows of identical houses are set on generously spaced lots. A few more substantial houses for superintendents, a doctor, and a store manager added some variety and made clear the social hierarchy of this community. TCI supplied jobs, houses, churches, schools, and a commissary for miners and their families. In 1952, TCI sold the camp houses to residents. Once mining activity ceased, this former company village became a suburban neighborhood.

"Coal mine at Lewisburg, Alabama. Some of the settlers on homesteads work here."
Photograph by Arthur Rothstein, February 1937.
Courtesy LOC-FSA.

The Sloss-Sheffield Steel and Iron Company operated the Lewisburg coal mines and coke ovens until the 1950s. Coke produced at the Lewisburg plant fueled the company's North Birmingham coke and chemical plant, established in 1918 and still operated by Sloss Industries. The Mary Lee Railroad ran from the Lewisburg mine to the chemical plant.

In the photograph, *above*, precut timbers to build the underground mining chambers are piled, *left*. The wooden superstructure is a coal washing facility. The hillside, *to the left*, is composed of mine tailings, residual materials of the industrial process.

"Coming out of the mine. Birmingham, Alabama."
Photograph by Arthur Rothstein, February 1937.
Courtesy LOC-FSA.

During the 1930s, mines operated on a reduced schedule, initially three days a week. Often, miners managed a full shift's work every two weeks.

"Coal miners. Birmingham, Alabama."
Photograph by Arthur Rothstein, February 1937.
Courtesy LOC-FSA.

BETTER HOUSING FOR INDUSTRIAL WORKERS

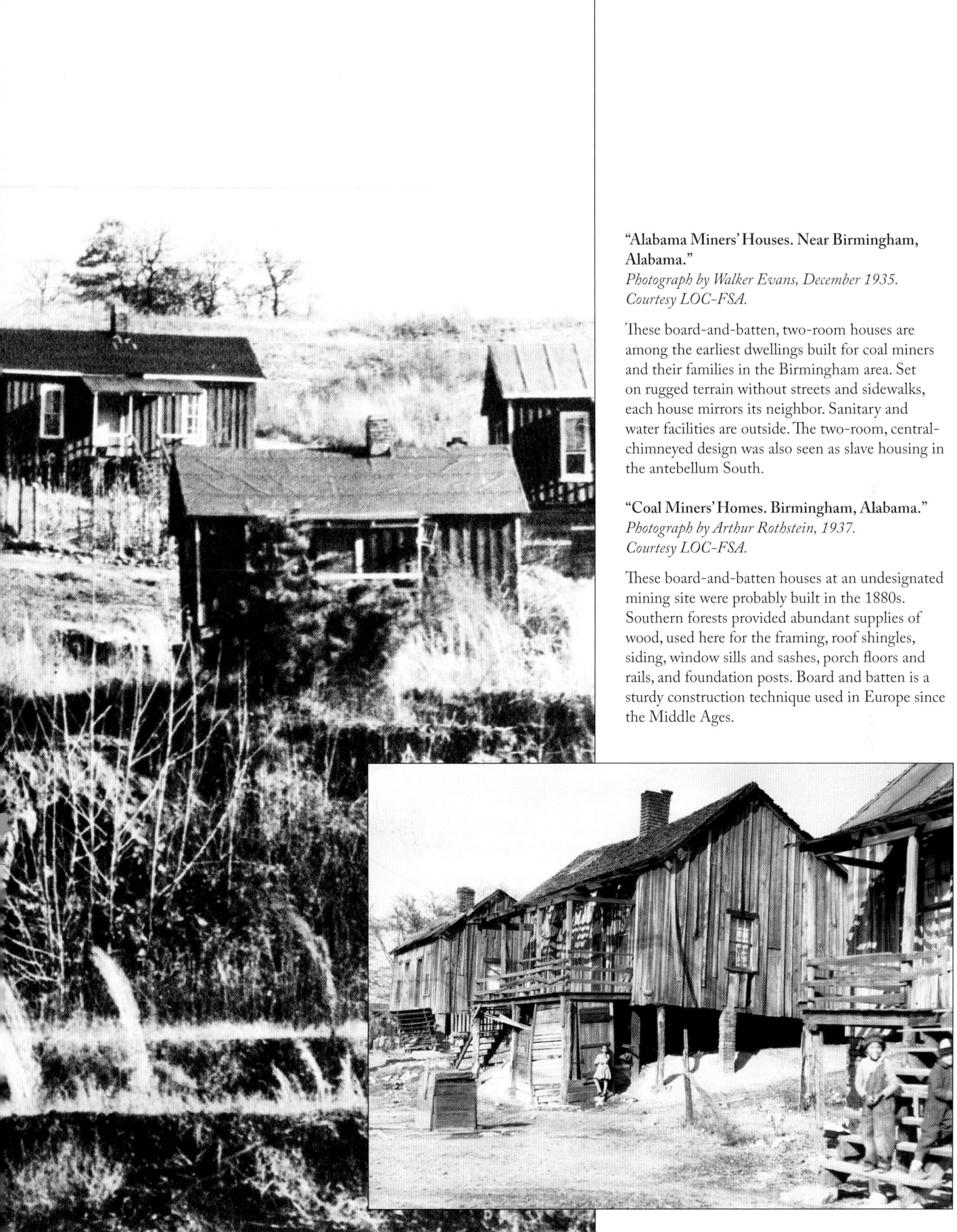

"Alabama Miners' Houses. Near Birmingham, Alabama."
Photograph by Walker Evans, December 1935.
Courtesy LOC-FSA.

These board-and-batten, two-room houses are among the earliest dwellings built for coal miners and their families in the Birmingham area. Set on rugged terrain without streets and sidewalks, each house mirrors its neighbor. Sanitary and water facilities are outside. The two-room, central-chimneyed design was also seen as slave housing in the antebellum South.

"Coal Miners' Homes. Birmingham, Alabama."
Photograph by Arthur Rothstein, 1937.
Courtesy LOC-FSA.

These board-and-batten houses at an undesignated mining site were probably built in the 1880s. Southern forests provided abundant supplies of wood, used here for the framing, roof shingles, siding, window sills and sashes, porch floors and rails, and foundation posts. Board and batten is a sturdy construction technique used in Europe since the Middle Ages.

"Home of Negro Family. Birmingham, Alabama."
Photograph by Arthur Rothstein, 1937. Courtesy LOC-FSA.

This two-room company house with "lean-to" extension at the back and a narrow porch at the front was probably built around 1900 to provide living quarters for two miners and their families.

The two front doors at 320 and 322 are screened. The clapboard (pronounced "'klabird'") siding and the rolled tar paper roof have been recently repaired and concrete steps poured, evidence of company crews fixing up the rental units. The porch has swings and decorative turned columns. The windows have shades and curtains.

"General store for iron ore miners. Muscoda, Alabama."
Photograph by Arthur Rothstein, February 1937. Courtesy LOC-FSA.

Companies provided not only housing for workers but also stores where they purchased goods with company scrip known as "clacker."

The company store (also known as the commissary) served as gathering place, pay office, post office, bill-collection office, and shopping center, handling everything from workers' tools to housewives' non-essentials—fuses and boots, food and furniture, clothing and laces. The hillside behind the commissary is stripped of its mineral resources.

"Gas Station and Miners' Houses. Lewisburg, Alabama."
Photograph by Walker Evans, December 1935.
Courtesy LOC-FSA.

Dominating this scene of identical miners' houses set along a narrow road are the Sloss benzol (a hometown-produced fuel) station and the power transmission lines that extend to the adjacent coal mine on the hillside behind the houses. The houses are one-room, board-and-batten structures with rear lean-to extensions and front porches. The trim is crisp and white, identifying them as company houses. They may be electrified. The road is surfaced with crushed rock.

"A Street in Brookside, Alabama, the small mining town where many of the Mt. Olive homesteaders formerly lived."
Photograph by Arthur Rothstein, February 1937.
Courtesy LOC-FSA.

The Brookside community grew up adjacent to Sloss coal mines, which attracted area farmers and scores of immigrants from Eastern Europe. St. Nicholas Russian Orthodox Church, established in 1894, built this frame church with Byzantine-style copper dome in 1914. In the 1930s, St. Nicholas sat along a dirt road, today's Church Street, adjacent to a heavily stripped hillside.

Palmerdale Homesteads

The first Birmingham homestead opened for occupancy in January 1936 at Palmerdale to the northeast of the city. Here, along the Birmingham to Oneonta Road, a 690-acre dairy farm became the setting for the Palmerdale farms. Under contract to the government, a local man built the initial 40 four- and six-room frame and brick farmhouses. Lots varied in size from 1½ to 6 acres.

In addition to the houses, the government financed a combined school and community center and a cooperative grocery store. Resettlement Administration staff leased the houses to the occupants until 1940, when all 75 houses constructed by the government were sold to tenants. Local records indicate the houses sold for $1,500 to $2,600 each. Government records indicate a unit cost of $9,205 with $938,865 as the total cost of building the community.

In June 1936 and February 1937, as the Palmerdale homesteads neared completion, the Washington staff of the Resettlement Administration sent photographers Carl Mydans and Arthur Rothstein to document the newly built crisp white cottages and Colonial Revival style houses. They also photographed family members at work on the farmsteads. Interviews with residents indicate that in-laws and children as well as hired staff contributed the farm labor necessary to cultivate the generous acreage provided by the government.

"Five room house, Southern colonial style, at the Palmerdale Homesteads near Birmingham, Alabama."
Photograph by Carl Mydans, June 1936.
Courtesy LOC-FSA.

"Plowing a field at Palmerdale, Alabama. New homesteads in the background."
Photograph by Arthur Rothstein, February 1937.
Courtesy LOC-FSA.

"Some of the children who are now residents of the Palmerdale Homesteads, Alabama."
Photograph by Arthur Rothstein, February 1937.
Courtesy LOC-FSA.

"Working in garden at Palmerdale Homesteads, Alabama. New homesteads in background."
Photograph by Arthur Rothstein, February 1937.
Courtesy LOC-FSA.

"Five Room Southern colonial style house at Palmerdale Homesteads near Birmingham, Alabama."
Photograph by Carl Mydans, June 1936.
Courtesy LOC-FSA.

"Backyards and houses of the Palmerdale Homesteads near Birmingham, Alabama."
Photograph by Carl Mydans, June 1936.
Courtesy LOC-FSA.

"Palmerdale Homestead boys working a watermelon patch near their house. Alabama."
Photograph by Carl Mydans, June 1936.
Courtesy LOC-FSA.

"Five room house and family at the Palmerdale Homesteads near Birmingham, Alabama.
Photograph by Carl Mydans, June 1936.
Courtesy LOC-FSA.

"One of the Palmerdale Homesteads near Birmingham, Alabama."
Photograph by Carl Mydans, June 1936.
Courtesy LOC-FSA.

Greenwood Homesteads

Birmingham landscape professional William Holmquist laid out the Greenwood community's roads, houses, and related buildings; the cooperative store; and the school-community center. The former 409-acre Martin farm site, several miles south of Bessemer, included flat lands and hilly topography that was extensively terraced to improve drainage. The floodplains of Rice Creek were "reserved" as a central woodland and open space. Septic tanks and field lines and a water system were installed. D. H. Greer designed 83 four-, five-, and six- bedroom homes and the multipurpose barns that served as garages, chicken houses, and feed and tool sheds. Coal houses were also built, as the burning of coal provided heat for the residences. The homes were set on three- to five-acre plots subdivided so that each parcel received as much tillable land as possible. The pastures and chicken yards were fenced and ready for use when the first tenants moved in on April 1, 1936. The Greenwood Homesteads were completed during 1937 and houses sold to residents and others beginning in 1940, with the compounded rent paid deducted from the purchase price.

Arthur Rothstein photographed Greenwood. His photographs reveal the stark newness of the community and its lack of landscaping. The roads across the red clay fields were screened with chert but became mud when it rained. The well-insulated homes featured flush toilets, laundry heaters that provided hot water for the stove, and automatic washing equipment on the screened back porch—all amenities that set new standards for rural Alabama living.

"The new house now occupied by the Chesser family at Greenwood Homesteads, Alabama."
Photograph by Arthur Rothstein, February 1937.
Courtesy LOC-FSA.

"Andy Smith's home at Greenwood Homesteads, Alabama."
Photograph by Arthur Rothstein, February 1937.
Courtesy LOC-FSA.

"Terraced fields at Greenwood Homesteads to prevent soil erosion. Alabama."
Photograph by Arthur Rothstein, February 1937.
Courtesy LOC-FSA.

"Mr. Chesser unloading some of his farming implements at the barn on his new homestead. Greenwood, Alabama."
Photograph by Arthur Rothstein, February 1937.
Courtesy LOC-FSA.

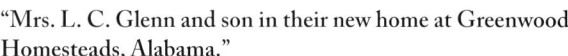

"Mrs. L. C. Glenn and son in their new home at Greenwood Homesteads, Alabama."
Photograph by Arthur Rothstein, February 1937.
Courtesy LOC-FSA.

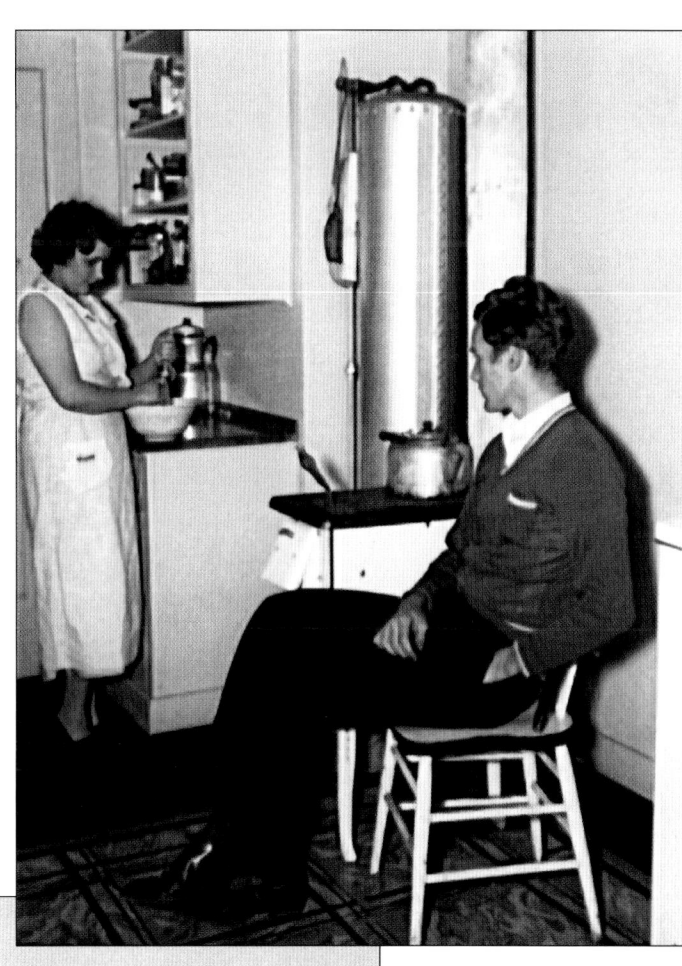

"Andy Smith and wife in their new home at Greenwood Homesteads, Alabama."
Photograph by Arthur Rothstein, February 1937.
Courtesy LOC-FSA.

"Mr. and Mrs. Andy Smith in the kitchen of their new home at Greenwood Homesteads, Alabama."
Photograph by Arthur Rothstein, February 1937.
Courtesy LOC-FSA.

"Greenwood Homesteads Community, Alabama."
Photograph by Arthur Rothstein, February 1937.
Courtesy LOC-FSA.

Moving Out and In

In February 1937, with 260 of the Birmingham homesteads completed and being offered to residents, Arthur Rothstein came to photodocument the new government-built homes and the homes from which the homesteaders moved.

John Beecher, who managed the Birmingham program, told a local news reporter, "It is not entirely a matter of getting people out of dilapidated shacks. In many cases it is not so much a question of leaving a deplorable housing condition as a chance to get out where they can have adequate garden space, and a chance for children to enjoy the advantages of country life." All applicants had to have stable employment in the mines and mills or commercial establishments sufficient to sustain the enterprise and to permit payment of a reasonable occupancy charge, he noted. Some of Rothstein's photographs were included in local news articles published April 25, 1937.

"Home of Noah Johnson of Fairfield, Alabama. The Johnson family will move to Mt. Olive Homesteads, Alabama."
Photograph by Arthur Rothstein, February 1937.
Courtesy LOC-FSA.

"Former home of George F. Spence of Brookside, Alabama. Mr. Spence now lives at Mt. Olive Homesteads, Alabama."
Photograph by Arthur Rothstein, February 1937.
Courtesy LOC-FSA.

"The backyard of Wesley H. Vickrey's present home in Wylam, Alabama. The Vickrey family will move to Mt. Olive Homesteads, Alabama."
Photograph by Arthur Rothstein, February 1937.
Courtesy LOC-FSA.

"Brookside miner's children, will move to Mt. Olive Homesteads."
Photograph by Arthur Rothstein, February 1937.
Courtesy LOC-FSA.

"Home of C. L. Earle. Fairfield, Alabama. This house is being vacated. The family is moving to Mt. Olive, Alabama."
Photograph by Arthur Rothstein, February 1937.
Courtesy LOC-FSA.

"The Eargle Family moving their household goods out of their home at Fairfield, Alabama. They will become homesteaders at Mt. Olive, Alabama."
Photograph by Arthur Rothstein, February 1937.
Courtesy LOC-FSA.

"The Eargle family moving out of their old home at Fairfield, Alabama. They will become homesteaders of Mt. Olive, Alabama."
Photograph by Arthur Rothstein, February 1937.
Courtesy LOC-FSA.

"Mrs. Wesley Vickrey, who will move to a new home at Alabama's Mt. Olive Homesteads. Wylam, Alabama."
Photograph by Arthur Rothstein, February 1937.
Courtesy LOC-FSA.

"Present home of Wesley Vickrey of Wylam, Alabama. Mr. Vickrey and his family will soon move to a new house at Mt. Olive, Alabama."
Photograph by Arthur Rothstein, February 1937.
Courtesy LOC-FSA.

Mount Olive Homesteads

Homesteads on the 512-acre Mount Olive tract, mistakenly called the "Gardendale Tract" by federal officials, also ranged from three to five acres. Agricultural experts devised the proposed planting plans: one third of the acreage of each homestead was to be devoted to pasture, one third to hay or feed crops, and one third to vegetable gardens, potatoes, or other truck crops. In addition to a four- to six-room house, each homestead was equipped with a combination barn and garage as well as cow pastures and chicken yards. William Holmquist laid out the new community. D. H. Greer designed the facilities.

The first five units of Mount Olive's 75 project homes were ready for occupancy in January 1937. For months before the opening, housing applicants by the hundreds poured into the Birmingham office. According to a survey by property tax officials, most families selected came from respectable industrial neighborhoods and rural areas, not from slum districts. Local newspaper accounts of the era estimated the average cost per family unit as $6,500; federal sources reported to the U.S. Congress a cost of $8,242 per unit with a total cost for the 75 homesteads and other community improvements of $618,162.

Arthur Rothstein photographed the Mount Olive homesteads, which are near Gardendale, today a northern suburb of Birmingham, in February, March, and April of 1937.

"House of Mt. Olive, Alabama."
Photograph by Arthur Rothstein, February 1937.
Courtesy LOC-FSA.

"Houses of Mt. Olive Homesteads, Alabama."
Photograph by Arthur Rothstein, February 1937.
Courtesy LOC-FSA.

"David Taylor moving into his new home at Mt. Olive, Alabama."
Photograph by Arthur Rothstein, February 1937.
Courtesy LOC-FSA.

"Completed House at Mt. Olive, Alabama."
Photograph by Arthur Rothstein, March 1937.
Courtesy LOC-FSA.

"Completed house on the Mt. Olive Project, Alabama."
Photograph by Arthur Rothstein, March 1937.
Courtesy LOC–FSA.

"The Howard family moving into their new home at Mt. Olive, Alabama."
Photograph by Arthur Rothstein, February 1937.
Courtesy LOC–FSA.

"Kitchen in one of the Mt. Olive Homesteads, Alabama.
Photograph by Arthur Rothstein, April 1937.
Courtesy LOC–FSA.

"Interior of a Mt. Olive Homestead, Alabama."
Photograph by Arthur Rothstein, April 1937.
Courtesy LOC–FSA.

Rammed Earth Houses

At Mount Olive, government officials experimented with an ancient building medium known as rammed earth to build modern houses. The construction costs were dirt cheap. Dirt was dug from the project site and mixed with sand and water. The project director was Thomas Hibben Jr., an architect and engineer educated at Princeton University, the University of Pennsylvania, and in London and Paris. Well tutored in how historic buildings were built and with a special interest in low-cost housing, Hibben served as the chief engineer for the Resettlement Administration and the mastermind for the Birmingham experiment.

Hibben drew the plans and supervised the construction. His team of 14 men, hired from the relief rolls, perfected the rammed earth technique. It took them five weeks to build the first of seven houses and five days to build the last one. Hibben designed the houses in the International style with flat roofs and wide roof overhangs. Walls of dirt dug from the site and tamped into building forms were 9 feet high and 17 inches thick. The walls were coated with linseed oil and stuccoed or painted. The process required little equipment and was labor-intensive, a desirable quality at this time of large-scale unemployment.

Project director Thomas Hibben Jr. made photographs showing the construction of the rammed houses in March and April of 1937. His captions describe the techniques employed.

"Digging dirt used in rammed earth construction near Birmingham, Alabama."
Photograph by Thomas Hibben Jr., March 1937.
Courtesy LOC-FSA.

"The bulkheads are firmly braced so as to maintain vertical alignment."
Photograph by Thomas Hibben Jr., March 1937.
Courtesy LOC-FSA.

"After each three-inch layer has been tamped, another layer is spread in the form and work resumed."
Photograph by Thomas Hibben Jr., March 1937.
Courtesy LOC-FSA.

"Tampers used in rammed earth construction."
Photograph by Thomas Hibben Jr., April 1937.
Courtesy LOC-FSA.

"The workmen stand in the forms and knead the loose earth with tampers."
Photograph by Thomas Hibben Jr., 1937.
Courtesy LOC-FSA.

"The bolts are removed and the holes plugged with mortar."
Photograph by Thomas Hibben Jr., 1937.
Courtesy LOC-FSA.

"When one house has been completed the forms are moved to the next building site. Form sections should not be larger than can be handled by a crew of three or four men."
Photograph by Thomas Hibben Jr., 1937.
Courtesy LOC-FSA.

"Rammed earth construction near Birmingham, Alabama."
Photograph by Thomas Hibben Jr., 1937.
Courtesy LOC-FSA.

"Whitewashing rammed earth house."
Photograph by Thomas Hibben Jr., 1937.
Courtesy LOC-FSA.

"Rammed earth house at Mt. Olive, Alabama."
Photograph by Arthur Rothstein, March 1937.
Courtesy LOC-FSA.

"Rammed earth house near Birmingham, Alabama."
Photograph by Thomas Hibben Jr., 1937.
Courtesy LOC-FSA.

"Rammed earth House at Mt. Olive, Alabama."
Photograph by Arthur Rothstein, March 1937.
Courtesy LOC-FSA.

"Rammed earth house near Birmingham, Alabama."
Photograph by Thomas Hibben Jr., 1937.
Courtesy LOC-FSA.

"Rammed earth house at Mt. Olive, Alabama."
Photograph by Arthur Rothstein, March 1937.
Courtesy LOC-FSA.

"Rammed earth house. Mt. Olive Tract, Birmingham, Alabama."
Photograph by Thomas Hibben Jr., 1937.
Courtesy LOC-FSA.

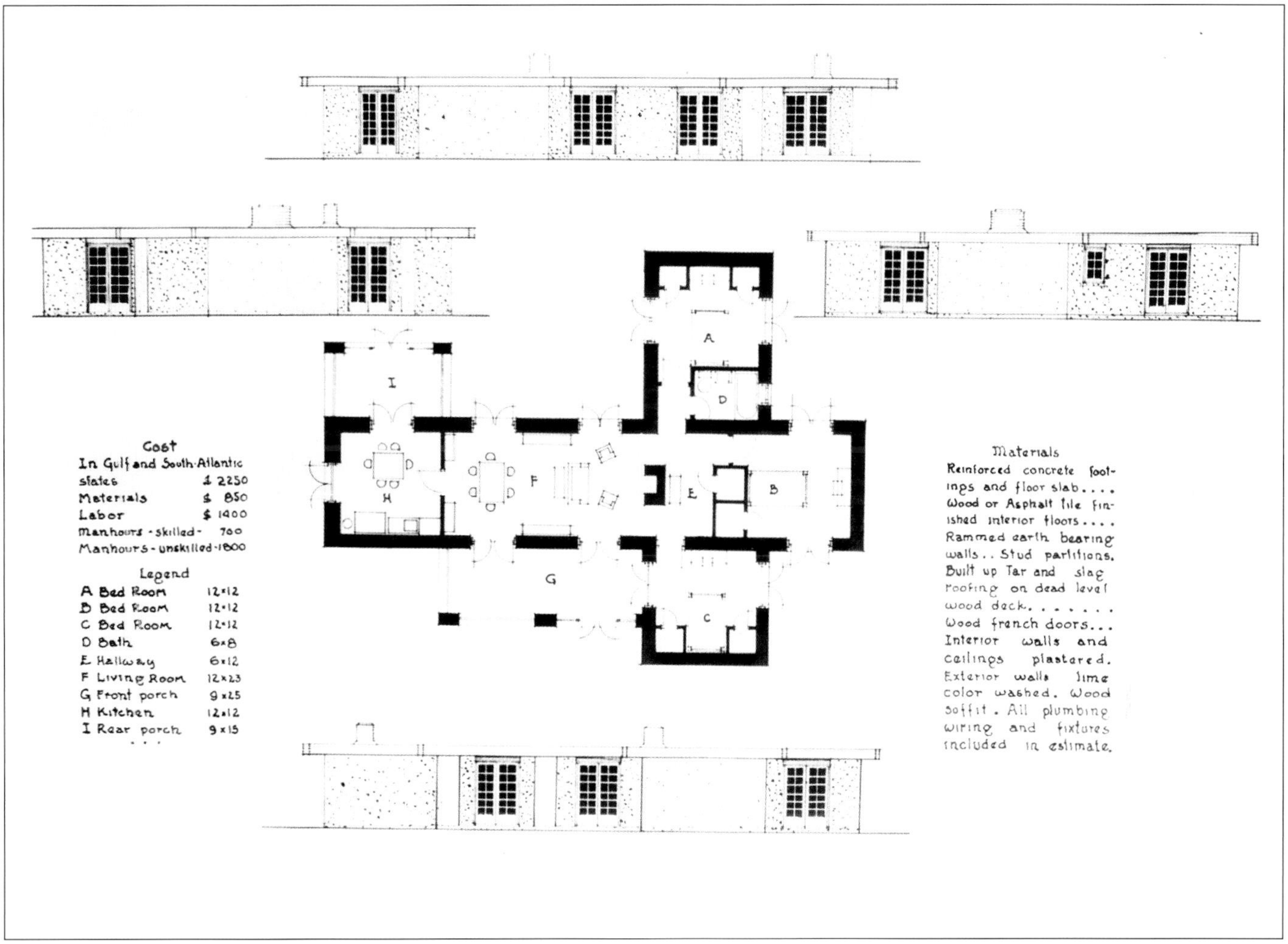

"Plan of rammed earth house, Alabama."
Photograph by Thomas Hibben Jr., 1937.
Courtesy LOC-FSA.

"Rammed earth pump house near Birmingham, Alabama," *left*.
Photograph by Thomas Hibben Jr., 1937.
Courtesy LOC-FSA.

"Barn constructed by rammed earth process. Mt. Olive, Alabama," *right*.
Photograph by Thomas Hibben Jr., 1937.
Courtesy LOC-FSA.

Slagheap Village–Cahaba Village at Trussville

The 750-acre site of the future federal housing project at Trussville included an abandoned furnace, several coke ovens, 60 company houses, and an immense slag pile. Proving unsuitable for redevelopment as farms, it remained vacant for three years after purchase as a subsistence homestead site. A local committee headed by the far-sighted developer Robert Jemison Jr., coal operator Charles DeBardeleben, and Jefferson County farm agent J. F. Lies convinced Resettlement Administration officials to redevelop the site as a federally sponsored "greenbelt" town through a new RA program initiated in 1936. Greenbelt, Maryland; Greenhills, Ohio; and Greendale, Wisconsin are other similar federal ventures.

Officially listed as Slagheap Village when construction began in July 1936, the project was renamed Cahaba Village for the wide greenbelt of parklands along the Cahaba River that formed the new community's eastern spine and gave it cohesion. Green space also extended along a 1,200-foot mall through the tree-lined village. A school and community facilities defined one edge of the village green, which continued to the parklands along the river. These extensive open spaces safeguarded the water supply, provided natural areas for recreation, and buffered the village from future encroaching and nonconforming developments.

Birmingham landscape architect William Kessler, who had earlier worked with national land planners employed by Jemison & Co. on developments such as Mountain Brook, designed the community, including all the bells and whistles of what was then considered top-notch planning.

Development work included construction of a waterworks, sewage disposal plant, utilties installation, street and sidewalk paving, curbs, gutters, 3 public buildings, and 287 dwelling units including 44 duplexes. Project architect D. H. Greer drew a dozen plans for the brick and frame houses, varying styles and materials. California redwood and TCI steel shingles were construction staples. While construction labor came from relief rolls, government inspectors insisted upon quality work.

Upon completion on April 1, 1938, the Cahaba Village was among the largest of the federally built new towns in terms of numbers of homes built, and among its finest. The total project cost was $2.7 million for the 287 units valued

"Scene at Slagheap Village, Alabama."
Photograph by Arthur Rothstein, February 1937.
Courtesy LOC-FSA.

at $9,619 each. Residents, who eventually purchased their homes in the well-planned town, developed a strong sense of community.

When Trussville incorporated in 1947, the federal project became a part of the town. Project houses were sold to tenants and others. The water, natural gas, and park systems were acquired by the new government.

Arthur Rothstein photographed the community in February of 1937 as the sewage disposal plant and early houses were under construction.

"Construction of the sewage disposal plant. Slagheap Village."
Photograph by Arthur Rothstein, February 1937.
Courtesy LOC-FSA.

"Painting one of the new houses for industrial and white collar workers of Birmingham. Slagheap Village, Alabama."
Photograph by Arthur Rothstein, February 1937.
Courtesy LOC-FSA.

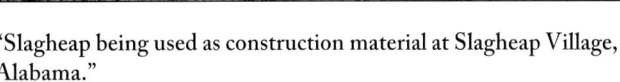

"Slagheap being used as construction material at Slagheap Village, Alabama."
Photograph by Arthur Rothstein, February 1937.
Courtesy LOC-FSA.

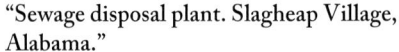

"Sewage disposal plant. Slagheap Village, Alabama."
Photograph by Arthur Rothstein, February 1937.
Courtesy LOC-FSA.

"One of the new houses at Slagheap Village, Alabama."
Photograph by Arthur Rothstein, February 1937.
Courtesy LOC-FSA.

Other Housing Ventures

Many New Deal initiatives attempted to stabilize the nation's existing housing stock, encourage home construction, and promote home ownership. The Federal Housing Administration established government support for long-term home mortgages. From 1934 to 1938, Birmingham developer Robert Jemison Jr. headed the Alabama office and sought to convince bankers that government-guaranteed mortgages would encourage well-designed new home construction.

The U.S. Congress also passed legislation to construct government-owned rental housing in major cities. The initial act was modified and expanded as the Housing Act of 1937, which provided for the establishment, through state law, of local public housing authorities to build, own, and operate the housing.

In Birmingham, the Public Works Administration (PWA), a federal agency that funded construction of massive public buildings and projects, funded the first two "slum clearance projects": the Smithfield Court Public Housing Project and the Elyton Village Housing Project.

Intended to provide "low cost, low rent" housing options, Smithfield Court served black tenants, and Elyton Village, white. Smithfield Court's 540 units of two to five rooms each were built for $2.5 million; Elyton Village's 860 units in 110 row houses and four apartment buildings cost $4.25 million. Birmingham architect D. O. Whilldin served as project architect, and William Holmquist was the landscape architect and planner for both projects.

The Smithfield Court project is a seven-square-block site that fronts 8th Avenue North and abuts Parker High School. It is the only Birmingham project to be featured in the PWA's survey of its best projects nationwide. The Beaux-Arts style site plan maximized the use of open space. The low-scale row houses occupied 27 percent of the total land area, and open space is reserved for a recreational commons, playgrounds, gardens, and walking paths. In 1938, First Lady Eleanor Roosevelt came to town for the parade down 8th Avenue that opened the new public housing venture.

The Housing Act of 1937 would provide further federal support for privately developed housing, by offering mortgage subsidies to private developers to construct large apartment complexes for persons of modest incomes. The Redmont Gardens and Park Lane Apartments in Mountain Brook would be among the projects using this program.

Open Space with Surrounding Row Houses, Smithfield Court Housing Project.
Photograph published in Public Buildings: A Survey of Projects Constructed by Federal and Other Governmental Bodies Between the Years 1933 and 1939 with the Assistance of the Public Works Administration, *1939. Courtesy BPL Government Documents Department.*

Aerial View, Smithfield Court Housing Project, Designed 1935–1938, Smithfield Neighborhood, Birmingham.
Photograph published in Public Buildings: A Survey of Projects Constructed by Federal and Other Governmental Bodies Between the Years 1933 and 1939 with the Assistance of the Public Works Administration, *1939. Courtesy BPL Government Documents Department.*

Community Building, Now Bethlehem House, 8th Avenue North, Smithfield Court Housing Project.
Rendering from the Postcard Collection, BPL Archives.

BETTER HOUSING FOR INDUSTRIAL WORKERS

May 21, 1936.

Hon. Franklyn D. Roosevelt, President,
United States of America,
At the White House,
Washington, D. C.,

Dear Mr. President:

      We of Birmingham, Alabama, are deeply interested in the low rental housing program of your Administration which is being carried on by the Housing Division of the P. W. A. It offers at present the only way by which those of our people, whose inadequate earnings would not otherwise allow it, may enjoy even a minimum standard of decency, sanitation and comfort in housing.

      Fortunate indeed do we count ourselves in that one such project, for negroes, is now being constructed here. For some six hundred families of our forty (40%) per cent negro population, this project when completed will mean more than we dare to express in words and the entire community, the taxpayers in every walk of life, will be benefitted by it; they will profit in health, happiness, improved citizenship and in dollars and cents.

      We have twenty-two blighted areas within our City, a consolidated report on which has just been completed and copy forwarded to Washington today. The Wagner Bill - S. 4426 - when enacted into law will place us in position to deal with and correct these thoroughly bad and economically disastrous conditions and we ask that you give your active support to the early passage of that measure.

                              Respectfully,

                              President of the Commission.

Housing Letter, James M. Jones Jr., City Commission President, to Franklin D. Roosevelt, May 21, 1936.
James M. "Jimmie" Jones Papers, File #1007, folder #5.2. BPL Archives.

Elyton Village, Graymont Avenue–
3rd Avenue West.
Photograph 1940, Birmingham News
Photograph Collection, BPL Archives.

Elyton Village, Graymont Avenue–
3rd Avenue West.
Photograph 1940, Birmingham News
Photograph Collection, BPL Archives.

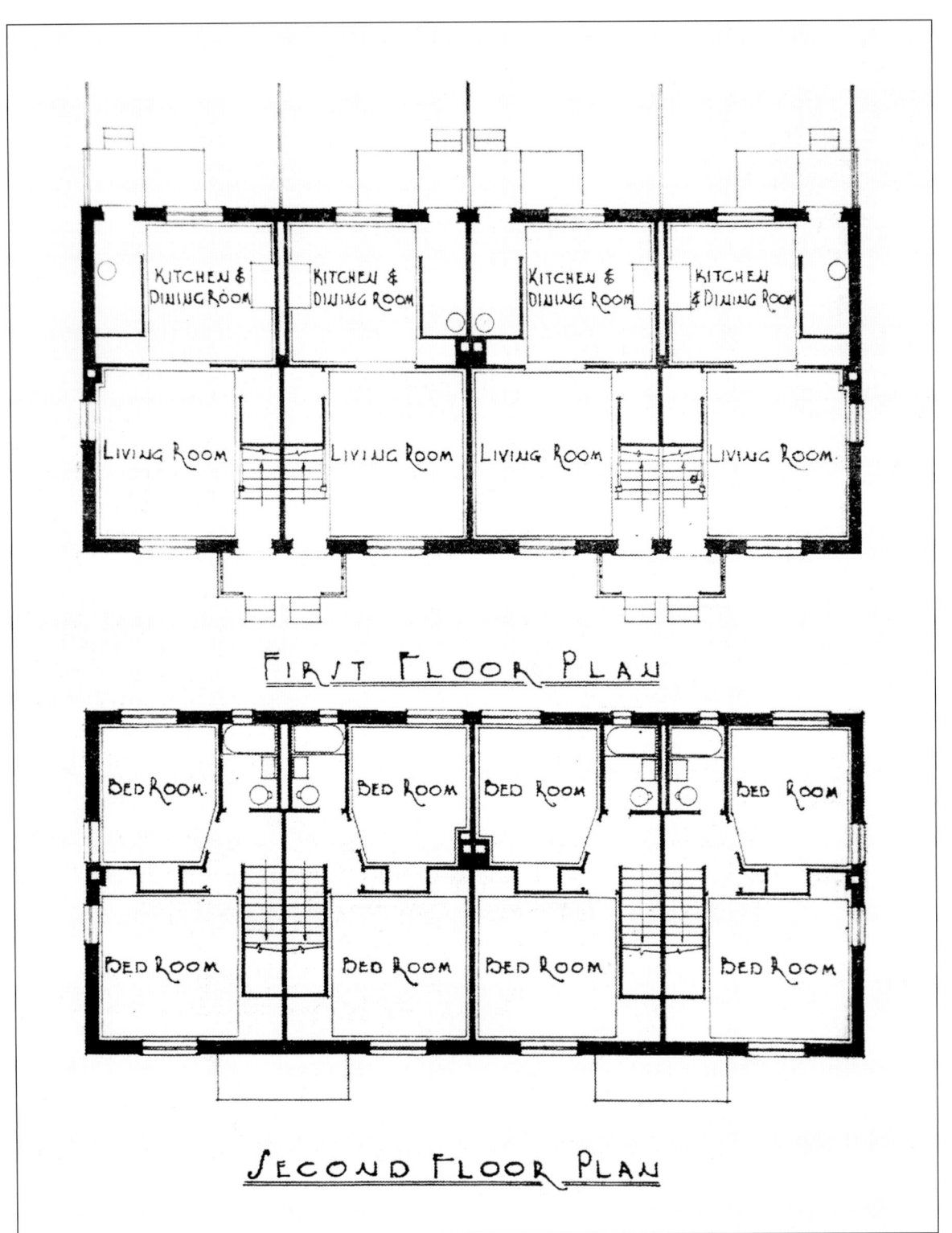

Floor Plans, First and Second Floors, Elyton Village.
Photograph published in "Families Will Move into Fairyland–Elyton Village," Birmingham Post, *1 January 1939. Clipping Files (Housing Authority of Birmingham District).*
Courtesy BPL Southern History Department.

Park Lane Apartments.
Photograph by A. C. Keily, 1950s.
Courtesy BPL Archives.

"**Park Lane Apartments, Inc. Mountain Brook, Alabama.**"
"276 Modern Fireproof Units consisting of 96 one bedroom, 168 two bedroom, and 12 bungalow apartments. Located over the mountain, in clean, cool Mountain Brook. Only twenty minutes from downtown Birmingham. Complete shopping and recreational facilities within walking distance."
Postcard published by Park Lane Apartments, 1949.
Courtesy the collection of Steve Gilmer, What's On Second?.

★★ USA ★★ WORK PROGRAM WPA.
Artist unknown, photolithograph, 1936.
Courtesy National Archives, Publications of the U.S. Government.

CHAPTER FIVE
JOBS FOR THE JOBLESS:
THE WORKS PROGRESS ADMINISTRATION (WPA)

Works Progress Administration (WPA) funds were given not only to counties and their departments of public health and public welfare, but also to cities, school boards, park boards, as well as the state highway department, archives, department of health, and geological survey for work in individual counties. Total federal allocations were tracked by state. Discovering what happened at the local level is a challenge.

WPA funds were for wages only. Local funds provided materials and a match if required. In today's dollars, a local worker paid $6.00 a day on a road building project would earn the equivalent weekly salary of $470. WPA jobs were not full-time jobs, nor were they permanent jobs. They did pay well.

WPA projects for Jefferson County are identified on index cards preserved on microfilm in the Birmingham Public Library Archives. From transcription of the microfilm, the following list of major projects and total expenditures has been compiled. While the index cards do not always identify individual projects, they do present the fullest picture available of the WPA's employment relief efforts here.

WPA Allocations in Jefferson County, 1935-1941

Categories	Millions of Dollars
City Streets	6.8
County Roads	5.2
Public Welfare	4.9
Public Buildings/Administration	4.9
Schools	4.5
Parks	3.7
Industrial Waterworks	3.5
Drainage/Sanitary Sewers	2.9
Public Health	1.9
State and Federal Highways	1.0
Military	0.7
Aviation	0.6
Total Allocation	$40.6 million*

* $637 million in today's dollars (A dollar in 1935 is worth $15.69 in purchasing power in 2009.)

WPA Project Cards.
Prints from microfilm.
Courtesy BPL Archives.

JOBS FOR THE JOBLESS 73

City Streets $6.8 million

- Improve streets in Birmingham, Bessemer, Cahaba Village at Trussville, Fairfield, Homewood, Leeds, Lipscomb, Irondale, Tarrant, and Warrior.
- Improve streets, including grading, surfacing, constructing sidewalks, curbs, gutters, and necessary drainage work. Surfacing materials include tar, tar and slag, slag, bitumen, concrete, and brick.
- Repair brick pavement, taking up paving and relaying brick on sand cushions.
- Produce slag for base material, bitumen, and concrete material for use on WPA projects, operating "borrow" pits and chert pits.
- Resurface alleys.
- Beautify public drives.
- Set street markers at intersections on city-owned property. *The Birmingham city engineer provided the specifications and supervised the project.*

County Roads $5.2 million

- Improve roads, grading, draining, surfacing, straightening, widening, constructing, and reconstructing bridges and culverts on county and privately owned property. Work on private property includes detours, drainage ditches, and cleaning roadsides.
- Bridge construction and repair.

State and Federal Highways $1.0 million

- Improve U.S. 31 including surfacing and shoulders.
- Grade, drain, and improve U.S. 31 from North Birmingham to Lewisburg, 1936.
- **Improve U.S. 31** from Homewood to top of Shades Mountain, **operate borrow pits.**
- **Improve U.S. 11** on First Avenue from 85th Street to Cozy Corner.
- **Improve Third Avenue.**
- **Improve state highway from Avondale to Irondale,** operate borrow pits to produce materials.
- Improve county-owned road from Shades Tavern to Walkers Gap and from Green Springs to Avenue G in Birmingham.

Concrete Street Signs, *above.*
City of Birmingham engineering drawing from *The American City, May 1938.*
Courtesy BPL.
[Status: Some are extant.]

Street Surfacing, *right.*
Photographs from *The American City, November 1935.*
Courtesy BPL.

Drainage/Sanitary Sewers $2.9 million

- Citywide **storm water drainage and sanitary sewer construction** projects in Birmingham, Bessemer, Homewood, Leeds, and Tarrant City. Typical projects included excavating, cleaning, grussing, constructing manholes, drainage ditches, culverts, and retaining walls; deepening, widening and straightening banks, and shaping canals and ditches. Grade, clean, slope banks and rip-rap masonry for ditches.
- Projects mentioned by name:
    Cahaba River at Leeds, deepened, widened, straightened.
    Greenwood Homestead, drainage canals and ditches straightened and shaped.
    Village Creek Canal, widened and straightened.
    Sanitary sewers in Enon Ridge, Ensley, Hollywood sections of Homewood, Hyde Park Settlement, Milner Heights, Mountain Brook Estates, near Powderly, Titusville, Trotwood district, and Wylam.

74   DIGGING OUT OF THE GREAT DEPRESSION

Sewer Work on 18th Street.
Photograph 1930s.
Courtesy Alabama Department of Archives and History.

Bridge on U.S. 31 at Lakeshore Drive.
Photograph 1942.
Courtesy BPL Archives.
[Status: Extant.]

Public Buildings/Administration $4.9 million

Public Buildings and Grounds, $2 million

- Bessemer City Hall Addition and Auditorium.
- Completion of the Birmingham Municipal Auditorium.
- Improvements at Cedar Hill and Oak Hill Cemeteries.
- Slossfield Negro Youth Training Center; Administration, Clinic, Education, and Recreational Buildings *(North Birmingham)*.
- Snow Rogers Community Center *(near Gardendale)*.
- Birmingham City Street and Garbage Department Stable and Garage, 1940.
- Additions to Birmingham's Southside Jail.
- A community house and auditorium at East Lake.
- Municipal Building, Fairfield, 1940.
- Brick and stone jail, welfare building, fire station building, Leeds.
- Street decorations, permanent float chassis, costumes, and parade equipment to be used by sponsor (the City of Birmingham) in the decoration of streets and parks.

Public Administration, $2.9 million

- Conduct studies for the Housing Authority of the Birmingham District: 1. **A real property survey of the metropolitan area** of Birmingham, land use, land coverage and type, construction, condition, facilities, rental value, # of persons per room of dwelling units and structures. Data on family income within a limited area also collated and tabulated. Results will provide up-to-date information on substandard housing, vacancies, doubling up income levels, and other matters necessary for developing plans for low-rent housing and slum clearance as well as other types of zoning. 2. **A study of the demand for low-rent housing** in Birmingham, Bessemer, Brighton, Fairfield, Homewood, Irondale, Tarrant, and Jefferson County for the Housing Authority of the Birmingham District, cost $850,000.
- Inventory, catalog, index, and transcribe archival materials.
- Prepare maps of sanitary sewers, tunnels, water mains, service lines, manholes, and catch basins.
- Provide employment for needy professionals, educational and clerical persons who will assist in organizing library services for the Birmingham Public Library, indexing, typing cards, and copying records and reports.
- Prepare a study of juvenile delinquency.
- Index Jefferson County Circuit Court records, Sheriff's execution dockets, case records of the Court of Domestic Relations and Juvenile Court, and a record of prisoners received and discharged from the county jail, 1895–1935.
- For the county, prepare report on expenditures, 1921–1935; install a new record and procedure for taking and maintaining an inventory of equipment and supplies owned by the county.
- For the county, install a new record and procedure for real property evaluation for tax assessment purposes by preparing and revising records of real property, etc. 41% sponsor funds. *Today these tax assessor records, located at BPL Archives, provide researchers valuable documentation on historic properties, including photographs from the late 1930s.*

Military $.7 million

- **National Guard armories** were built at McLendon Park (the **Graymont Armory**) and Lewisburg. At the Municipal Airport, an administrative building, taxiways, and a hanger were built. Armory additions, truck sheds, and rifle ranges were also built at locations not identified.

Aviation $.6 million

- **Roberts Field** was improved and a hanger, shop, garage, groundwork, runways, and lighting were built at the **Birmingham Municipal Airport**. Airports were built at Bessemer and Warrior.

Waterworks $3.5 million

The Industrial Waterworks System

- Construct a Distribution Reservoir and Distribution Line for the Birmingham Industrial Water Supply System located in Jefferson County, near Mt. Pinson, and the opening and operating of a limestone quarry, stone crushers, and screens for furnishing stone and *[illegible]* for impounding the Dam for the above system located in Blount Co., near Inland. Quarry is a public quarry, work on public property in addition to projects specifically approved. No local match. Funded 12/35, 10/36, 4/37, 2/38.
- Construct water system for Pleasant Grove.
- Construct waterline to children's fresh air camp, located 7 miles south of Birmingham on Shades Mt.

"Birmingham's Industrial Water Supply."
Article from The American City, *May 1936.*
Courtesy BPL.

Graymont Armory, 210 Graymont Avenue West, McLendon Park.
Photograph 1949, from the Jefferson County Tax Assessor's Property Survey.
Courtesy BPL Archives.
[Status: Demolished.]

Bessemer City Hall Auditorium and Addition.
Photograph 1939, from the Jefferson County Tax Assessor's Property Survey, a survey funded by the WPA.
Courtesy BPL Archives.
[Status: Extant.]

Slossfield Community Center.
Photograph 1938, from the Jefferson County Tax Assessor's Property Survey.
Courtesy BPL Archives.

WPA workers also built and staffed the Administration, Clinic, Education, and Recreational Buildings at this North Birmingham site. Local industries provided additional funding for this center. [Status: Abandoned.]

Birmingham Municipal Airport.
Photograph by American Airways, 1930s.
Courtesy BPL Archives.

WPA workers improved the hanger and built runways and light towers. Prior to these improvements, planes landed in the field and loaded passengers and freight from the concreted area, *the light area in this photograph*. At the airport, the WPA also built National Guard facilities, *not shown in this photograph*.

JOBS FOR THE JOBLESS   77

Hillman Hospital Outpatient Clinic Building, completed 1939.
Photograph 1940.
Courtesy BPL Archives.
[Status: Demolished.]

Jefferson Hospital, dedicated 1940.
Photograph showing PWA project sign.
Courtesy BPL Archives.

In 1944, the University of Alabama entered into a 99-year contract with Jefferson County, builder of this hospital, for the lease of the Jefferson and Hillman Hospitals. [Status: Extant, now the Jefferson Tower at UAB Medical Center.]

Public Health $1.9 million

- Abandoned coal mines were sealed to prevent spillage into area water supplies.
- **Hillman Hospital Clinic** for charity patients was constructed and staffed by local physicians and nurses. $400,000. *Until the completion of the Jefferson Hospital (now Tower) in 1940 (funded by the Public Works Administration-PWA), Hillman was the principal hospital providing services to indigent persons in Jefferson County.*
- **TB clinics and the Sanatorium Building** *(the latter at today's Lakeshore Foundation in Homewood)* were constructed and staffed by needy nurses and doctors.
- Conduct a **public health education program**, lecturing before civic groups; promoting and organizing local study groups; preparing, delivering, and distributing copies of a series of radio health talks; preparing and distributing health pamphlets, posters, recordings for phonographs and radio use, and preparing and displaying health exhibits.
- Clean and spray vacant lots to **prevent mosquito and rodent breeding**.
- Prepare an inventory and **record of dogs** in Jefferson County, showing the names and addresses of owners, number and breed, sex and age, and date of immunization or inoculation against rabies. To aid in controlling and preventing rabies.
- Transcribe **birth and death records**.
- **Survey blighted areas** to determine cost of necessary sewers and health improvements.
- Investigate coagulation of sewage using salt.

Public Welfare $4.9 million

- **Sewing Rooms.** Provide employment for needy persons in the maintenance and operation of sewing rooms. Products will be distributed free of charge to charitable institutions, or to the needy. Approximately 20 hours per month will be spent in training in methods of childcare and household management, total allocations to Birmingham and Jefferson County, $3 million.
- **Make mattresses** by hand from government surplus cotton and ticking, distribute to needy families.
- **Weave rugs** and other household items for free distribution to charitable institutions.
- Renovate donated furniture to be given to needy families.
- Repair, renovate clothing, mattresses, tents, cots, shoes, household supplies, and goods donated by federal government and local public institutions.
- **Make toys and gifts** from purchased materials, $675,000, 1/36; make and repair cloth, wooden, and composition toys for free distribution in the City of Birmingham, 11/39, $343,404.
- County-wide. Furnish free home assistance in housework and care of children in the houses of the needy where the homemaker is totally or partially incapacitated because of ill health or confinement, or in case of temporary emergency, 8/38, $112,498.

Tuberculosis Sanatorium, Homewood, *left.*
Photograph 1938.
Courtesy BPL Archives.
[Status: Extant, now Lakeshore Rehabilitation Hospital.]

Medical and Dental Clinic, Lincoln Elementary School, *below left.*
Photograph by Birmingham View Co.
Courtesy BPL Archives.

Clinic in the Slossfield Hospital.
Photograph courtesy UAB Archives, University of Alabama at Birmingham.

The Slossfield Health Center provided pediatric clinics, health education, and training for black doctors and nurses.

Negro Women's Sewing Room.
Photograph 1930s, WPA District 8 Scrapbook and Photo Album, MS 1250.
Courtesy the Georgia Historical Society, Savannah, Georgia.

Similar rooms operated at 2831 N. 27th Street in Birmingham, at 10th Avenue and 34th Street North in Birmingham, and at 5 S. 19th Street in Bessemer.

White Women's Sewing Room.
Photograph 1930s, WPA District 8 Scrapbook and Photo Album, MS 1250.
Ccourtesy the Georgia Historical Society, Savannah, Georgia.

JOBS FOR THE JOBLESS

Parks $3.7 million

- **Oak Mountain State Park** *(for the Recreational Demonstration Area, not including the CCC improvements, these allocations to Jefferson and Shelby Counties, $.8 million)*
- **Birmingham Parks**, $1.7 million, improvements to Avondale, East Lake, Lane, McLendon, Woodrow Wilson, and 24 other parks, build 4 swimming pools, improve playgrounds, build 20 roller skating rinks, construct a community center in Central Park, improve Municipal Stadium *(Legion Field)*.
- Improve drainage and build masonry dams on the Roebuck Springs Golf Course *(Hawkins Park)*.
- Improve **parks throughout the city**, work includes construction of recreation facilities, shelter buildings, walks, bleacher seats, and baseball diamonds, surfacing tennis courts, opening quarries to produce materials for use in the project.
- Construct **fish hatchery basins** in Lane Park *(today's zoo ponds)*.
- Construct a **concrete shaft** and move and **erect Vulcan statue** in Park on Red Mountain, near Birmingham *(today's Vulcan Park)*.
- Fairfield, a **colored playground**, $60,000.
- To Birmingham, Bessemer, Homewood, Leeds, and Jefferson County funds for **park and playground staff**.

Community Center in Central Park, *right*.
Photograph by the Birmingham News.
Courtesy BPL Archives.
[Status: Extant with modifications.]

Fish Hatchery Basins in Lane Park, 1936–1937.
Photograph courtesy BPL Archives.
[Status: Extant as the ponds at the Birmingham Zoo.]

Playground Supervision, ACIPCO Park.
Photograph 1930s.
Courtesy BPL Archives.

The WPA provided annual funds to school and park boards to "employ needy persons to supervise and coordinate recreational activities, including recreational and leisure time leaders for games, sports, social activities, and training for recreational leadership."

Vulcan Monument in Vulcan Park, atop Red Mountain.
Photograph by O. V. Hunt, circa 1939.
Curtesy BPL Archives.

WPA funds paid for the labor to move and erect the Vulcan statue on Red Mountain and for extensive improvements to all Birmingham parks. [Status: Extant.]

Councill School, Auditorium Addition, *above.*
Photograph 1940, from the Jefferson County Tax Assessor's Property Survey.
Courtesy BPL Archives.
[Status: Extant.]

Rosedale School, Homewood.
Photograph 1959, from the Jefferson County Tax Assessor's Property Survey.
Courtesy BPL Archives.
[Status: Extant, formerly the Resource Learning Center (Shades Valley Annex), now the Islamic Academy of Alabama.]

McAdory High School Auditorium, McCalla.
Photograph 1948.
Courtesy Davis Architects, Inc.
[Status: Extant, renovated in 2006 by Davis Architects, the original architectural firm for the WPA-built school.]

Ramsay High School, Auditorium, Cafeteria, and Classroom Addition, *below.*
Photograph 1952.
Courtesy BPL Archives.
[Status: Extant.]

82 DIGGING OUT OF THE GREAT DEPRESSION

Playground, Graymont Elementary.
Photograph 1930s.
Courtesy Birmingham Board of Education Collection, BPL Archives.

Playground and athletic facilities were improved at schools throughout the county.

School Lunch, Industrial [Parker] High School Cafeteria.
Photograph by Birmingham View Co.
Courtesy Birmingham Board of Education Collection, BPL Archives.

WPA workers served school lunches "for needy students" throughout the county.

New Filing System for the Birmingham Board of Education Office.
Photograph by Birmingham View Co.
Courtesy BPL Archives.

Schools $4.5 million

- **Birmingham schools**, painting and repairs to all elementary and high schools; new construction of the Snow Rogers School and a community house; additions to Industrial High (Parker), Ramsay High (auditorium, cafeteria, classrooms), and West End High School (auditorium, cafeteria, and home economics wing); conversion of existing buildings for Tuggle, Lincoln, and South Highland Schools; additions to Barrett, Belview Heights, Councill, Curry, Gibson (amphitheatre seats), Graymont, Minnie Holman, Inglenook, Lakeview, Lincoln, 17th Avenue, 30th Street, Tuggle, Wilson, and Woodlawn Schools; WPA-NYA additions to Public School Buildings; facilities improvement at Alley, Baker, Councill, Gate City, Gorgas, and West End Schools; school lunch program, $2 million.
- **Jefferson County schools**, repairs to more than 135 schools: new schools at McAdory and Gardendale; additions to Riley, Gardendale, Huffman, and Hooper City Schools; improvements to grounds and athletic facilities, including landscaping, draining, constructing driveways, walkways, walls, steps, and curbs; cleaning, grubbing, excavating, installing drainage facilities, sodding, planting grass and shrubs; school lunch program, $1.7 million.
- **Fairfield**, repairs, additions to several schools, a new high school at 59th Street; athletic fields, stadium, bleacher seats at Fairfield High School.
- **Homewood**, construct Rosedale School.
- **Tarrant High School**, addition.
- **Warrior**, school auditorium, landscape grounds.
- **Alabama Boy's Industrial School** at Roebuck, additions to existing campus, $184,000.
- **Alabama Training School for Girls** at Chalkville, construction of a new campus, $506,631.
- Draining, grading, and landscaping school grounds at city and county schools.
- Improvements to **school playgrounds and athletic facilities**, including constructing bleacher seats, walks, landscaping, steps, backstops, tennis courts, and drives and operating quarries to produce materials for use on this project.
- **School lunch** program for needy students in Jefferson County, 1937–38, $54,435.
- Support to school administrative personnel.
- Bind, rebind, and repair books; make and repair window shades, renovate bus cushions, clean, scrape, sand, and varnish school furniture and equipment, plant shrubbery and trim trees on school grounds, repaint interior and replaster schools.

Chapter Six
Creating a City Beautiful:
WPA Beautification efforts

In the late 1930s, beautification of highways, entrances to towns and cities, town and city streets, schools, and farm and home grounds was administered under statewide beautification programs. Typically, the Works Progress Administration provided labor to supervise and plant. Local civic committees, garden club leaders, and professional park staff coordinated the projects, raised funds or received donations for the plant materials, and became responsible for the maintenance of the extensive plantings. Marion Thomas Brooks (1897–1977), a University of Kentucky–trained horticulturalist who took a summer course at Harvard University's horticultural program in 1922, administered the Alabama program most probably from 1936 to 1941, coordinating it statewide with the local sponsors. Brooks' scrapbooks, recently re-located in the Birmingham Botanical Gardens Library Archives, document the WPA Beautification program guidelines and many of the projects statewide. To support the efforts, Homer S. Fischer of the Alabama Cooperative Extension Service at Auburn prepared a series of 14 horticultural papers to help develop an appreciation of the importance of beautifying one's environment and the proper ways to grow, propogate, transplant, nurture, and handle pest control for the improvement programs. The use of native plants was strongly encouraged, as natives are more drought- and disease-tolerant.

The Birmingham Chamber of Commerce, the Exchange Club, and the federated garden clubs coordinated the Birmingham projects. Following upon Mobile and New Orleans' establishment of azalea trails (intended for economic development and to encourage tourists to stop and visit), Birmingham developed dozens of miles of roses along the highways and entrances to the city and also planted crape myrtle, dogwood, althea, wild hydrangea, vitex, spirea, abelia, iris, and jasmine along the roadways. By

Members of the Greater Birmingham Beautification Board, 1938 at the initial meeting of the board at the Tutwiler [Hotel], *far left*. Seated from left to right, Jessica Ingram, secretary; Mrs. C. F. Manly, Mrs. T. M. Francis, Erskine Ramsay, Mrs. J. Frank Parks, Dr. J. F. Hardin, chairman, and T. K. Byrne. Standing, left to right, M. Thomas Brooks, Robert Jemison Jr., Andrew Thomas, and Roy S. Marshall.
Photograph published in the Birmingham News, *1938. Brooks Scrapbooks, Archives and Rare Book Room, Birmingham Botanical Gardens Library.*

The *News* article indicates these individuals represent a cross section of Birmingham's industrial, commercial, and civic life that backs the beautification efforts. It is a blue ribbon committee, indeed. Jemison was the leading real estate developer; Erskine Ramsay a major industrialist, philanthropist, and chairman of the school board; Roy Marshall the longtime superintendent of Birmingham parks; and Brooks, the statewide WPA coordinator.

W.P.A. Beautification Office, Flomaton, *left*.
Photograph circa 1938.
Brooks Scrapbooks, Archives and Rare Book Room, Birmingham Botanical Gardens Library.

W.P.A. Beautification Office, Flomaton, *below*.
Photograph circa 1938.
Brooks Scrapbooks, Archives and Rare Book Room, Birmingham Botanical Gardens Library.

CREATING A CITY BEAUTIFUL

1937, more than 7,000 roses had been planted along the Bankhead Highway, the Florida Short Route (today's U. S. 280), and the Montgomery Highway. Roses cost ten cents each for two-year-old plants. In 1940, the Chamber of Commerce produced a colored motion picture, *Birmingham-The Industrial City Beautiful*, documenting beautification efforts. Motorcades and special tours and maps also showcased the massive efforts to "green" the traffic routes.

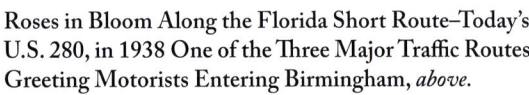

Roses in Bloom Along the Florida Short Route–Today's U.S. 280, in 1938 One of the Three Major Traffic Routes Greeting Motorists Entering Birmingham, *above.*
Photograph circa 1938.
Brooks Scrapbooks, Archives and Rare Book Room, Birmingham Botanical Gardens Library.

More than 7,000 rose bushes were purchased by a committee headed by T. K. Byrne and planted by WPA labor.

1800 Plants Donated by Joseph H. Abercrombie For Planting at the Lane Park Arboretum–Today's Birmingham Zoo.
Photograph circa 1938.
Brooks Scrapbooks, Archives and Rare Book Room, Birmingham Botanical Gardens Library.

The local committee arranged for donations of plant materials to supplement material raised and propagated in WPA-sponsored nurseries.

Crape Myrtle Trail, Birmingham, *left*.
Photograph circa 1938, Brooks Scrapbooks, Archives and Rare Book Room, Birmingham Botanical Gardens Library.

Crape myrtle trees were planted along Bush Boulevard, Edgewood Lake, in North Birmingham, from Hollywood to Mountain Brook Village, and along the Bessemer and Powderly boulevards.

Grading and Plantings, Tarrant City School, *right*.
Photograph circa 1938, Brooks Scrapbooks, Archives and Rare Book Room, Birmingham Botanical Gardens Library.

Planting Shrubs, Woodlawn High School, Birmingham, *left*.
Photograph circa 1938.
Brooks Scrapbooks, Archives and Rare Book Room, Birmingham Botanical Gardens Library.

Beds were prepared and shrubs planted by female workers at many school grounds.

Picture Page of WPA Projects.
No. 5. Italian born women, now living in the county, learn to become citizens under WPA supervision.
No. 6. A WPA monument, the four-lane Green Springs road looking north toward Birmingham, part of 795 miles constructed or improved by WPA in the county.
No. 7. A monument to WPA-Vulcan. Its rock park and setting is the pride of masons who built it.
No. 8. The Alabama State Training Schools for Girls, one of the most modern of its type in the nation.
No. 9. WPA workers molding some of the 14,534 street markers for Birmingham. Other cities have followed this method of street marking.
No. 10. Building the intricate forms for pouring concrete in the construction of the Fairfield City Hall.
Photographs from an undated Birmingham newspaper.
Brooks Scrapbooks, Archives and Rare Book Room, Birmingham Botanical Gardens Library.

This undated picture page of WPA project photographs is found in one of Thomas Brooks' scrapbooks of news clipping on statewide beautification projects.

CREATING A CITY BEAUTIFUL

Chapter Seven
Artists on Relief: A New Deal for the Arts

The New Deal provided jobs to all kinds of American workers, including artists. From 1933 to 1943, painters, sculptors, graphic designers, and art teachers received the standard white-collar wage to make and share their art. By law, works of art produced by artists on "relief" were to be displayed in public places, such as schools, libraries, courthouses, and post offices.

Painter Richard Coe, who served briefly as director of Alabama's federal art programs, captured their aspiration to create a new form of American art:

> The art spirit (art for art's sake) created in the nineteenth century is all well and good, but there is an art for the people. The government is doing its best to develop it by taking charge and giving work to artists to do art for the education and delight of the people. American art for American people is a slogan well worth heeding.... The modernistic era has passed. A 'new deal' in art has come in with all the other 'new deals.' The government has it in its power to create a good one.... We are an educated race and use painting as a useful purpose.
>
> Richard Coe quoted by Dolly Dalrymple, "Winner of Scholarship Returns on Visit," Birmingham News, 9 May 1934.

During 1933 and 1934, the earliest federal program, the Public Works of Art Project (PWAP), was funded through the Civil Works Administration and operated under the U.S. Treasury Department. The PWAP put thousands of artists to work nationwide. Locally, 12 prominent Alabama artists, including Coe as well as Frank Hartley Anderson, Martha Fort Anderson, Hannah Elliott, John Kelly Fitzpatrick, William Grant, Carrie Hill, and Sidney Van Sheck, produced oil portraits and paintings of public figures and local scenes, woodcuts, watercolors, murals, bronze plaques, and statues as well as special displays of their "relief" work. Perhaps the best-known PWAP project is the full-size statue of the beloved pastor of Third Presbyterian Church, the Reverend "Brother" Bryan still on display in Five Points South in Birmingham.

Birmingham Steel Mill.
Richard Blauvelt Coe (1904–1978, active in Birmingham 1934–1940). Oil on canvas, 1934. Signed and dated, center, verso: COE 34. Courtesy Montgomery Museum of Fine Arts, Montgomery, Alabama, Gift of the Artist, 1940.31.

This painting, which the editors believe to be of the still extant though not operating Sloss Furnace No. 2, hung in the Montgomery offices of Alabama's relief administrator, Thad Holt. Coe later transferred the painting to the Montgomery Museum of Fine Arts, then a federally supported museum that was actively acquiring the nucleus of its superb regional art collection.

Beginning in October 1934, the Treasury Department Section of Painting and Sculpture, later known as the Section of Fine Arts, commissioned art for new federal buildings. Two dozen new Alabama post offices, including those at Fairfield and Montevallo, were decorated under this program (*see table, at right*). Encouraged by the federal mandate to provide art that everyone might understand and enjoy, the local postmasters selected the themes, which most often reflected local historical and real-life scenes. Artists competed for these prestigious commissions.

In 1935, the Works Progress Administration (WPA) established the most ambitious cultural program: Federal Project Number One. Five "Federal One" divisions supported the arts: the Federal Art Project (FAP), the Federal Music Project (FMP), the Federal Theatre Project (FTP), the Federal Writers' Project (FWP), and the Historical Records Survey (HRS, originally part of the Writer's Project). All persons employed in these programs actually worked for the WPA. The programs were coordinated out of Washington and state government offices. Detailing the local scene, Birmingham artists recorded iron- and steel-making operations, African-American life, and the region's historical events.

Church Supper.
Frank Hartley Anderson (1891–1947, active in Birmingham 1909–1938). Woodcut, 1934. Collection of Lynn B. Williams Katz, Auburn, Alabama.
Published with the permission of Jordan Prince, Locust Valley, New York.

Frank Hartley Anderson's most highly acclaimed woodcut print, made in 1934 and exhibited at local and national shows, typifies the then-new trend to use native topics as subject matter for art works, particularly local and typical Southern subjects and especially African-American gatherings. Anderson founded the Southern Printmakers Society, which became a regional graphics art organization that set standards for prints and exhibited and sold them to growing numbers of patrons. His artist wife, Martha Fort Anderson, collaborated in many of his works, including providing sketches for this print. The scene, *above*, shows individuals grouped for a meal during which plates of hot biscuits are being served.

New Deal Artwork in Alabama Post Offices

Location	Title	Artist	Date	Medium
Alexander City (now in storage at City Hall)	*Cotton, Tobacco, and Wheat*	Franc Epping	1941	Terra cotta reliefs
Atmore	*The Letter Box*	Anne Goldthwaite*	1938	Oil on canvas
Bay Minette	*Removal of the County Seat from Daphne to Bay Minette*	Hilton Leech	1939	Oil on canvas
Brewton	*Logging*	John Von Wicht	1939	(Missing)
Carrollton (Post Office and Agricultural Building)	*Farm Scene with Senator Bankhead*	Stuart R. Purser	1943	Mural
Enterprise (now in the Public Library)	*Saturday in Enterprise*	Paul Arlt	1941	Tempera
Eutaw	*The Countryside*	Robert Gwathmey	1941	Oil on canvas
Fairfield	*Spirit of Steel*	Frank Hartley Anderson* and Martha Fort Anderson*	1938	Oil on canvas
Fort Payne	*Harvest at Fort Payne*	Harwood Steiger	1938	Oil on canvas (two panels)
Guntersville	*Indians Receiving Gifts from the Spanish*	Charles Russell Hardman	1947	Oil on canvas
Haleyville (now the Public Library)	*Reforestation*	Hollis Holbrook	1940	Mural (painted over)
Hartselle (now in the Hartselle Chamber of Commerce)	*Cotton Scene*	Lee R. Warthen	1941	Mural
Huntsville (Post Office and Courthouse)	*Tennessee Valley Authority*	Xavier Gonzalez	1937	Mural (several panels)
Luverne	*Cotton Field*	Arthur Getz	1942	Mural
Monroeville (Post Office and Agricultural Building)	*Harvesting*	Arthur Leroy Bairnsfather*	1939	Oil on canvas
Montevallo	*Early Settlers Weighing Cotton*	William S. McCall	1939	Oil on canvas
Oneonta (now the Blount County Courthouse Annex, Blount County Board of Education)	*Local Agriculture–A.A.A. 1939*	Aldis B. Browne	1939	Oil on canvas
Opp	*Opp*	Hans Mangelsdorf	1940	Wood relief (missing)
Ozark	*Early Industry of Dale County*	John Kelly Fitzpatrick*	1938	Oil on canvas
Phenix City (now the Public Library)	*Cotton*	John Kelly Fitzpatrick*	1939	Oil on canvas
Russellville	*Shipment of First Iron Produced in Russellville*	Conrad A. Albrizzio	1938	Fresco
Scottsboro	*Alabama Agriculture*	Constance Ortmayer	1940	Plaster bas-relief (three panels)
Tuscumbia	*Chief Tuscumbia Greets the Dickson Family*	Jack McMillen	1939	Mural
Tuskegee	*The Road to Tuskegee*	Anne Goldthwaite*	1937	Oil on canvas

*Alabama artist

Sources for the Post Office Mural Listing: "New Deal/WPA Art in Alabama," http://www.wpamurals.com/alabama.htm; Alabama Department of Archives and History, "New Deal Art in Alabama Post Offices and Federal Buildings," http://www.alabamamoments.state.al.us/sec49det.html.

Nearly every known local artist of the period participated, creating paintings, prints, murals, sculpture, and teaching aids. Quilters, basket and rug weavers, and those creating needle and other forms of folk art were also employed. WPA workers also staffed art centers and galleries, taught children's art classes, and arranged exhibitions. The Birmingham Public Library hosted many local and traveling displays. Special shows also featured the work of young artists at the Library, Birmingham-Southern College, Howard College (now Samford University), and the Federal Art Museum, then located in Henley School at 1700 Sixth Avenue North. Artists also gave lectures to groups on art and museum subjects, collected information about Alabama artists, and circulated materials in the public schools.

The best-known local WPA art projects are the large murals commissioned for libraries, schools, and the state fair. The mural at Woodlawn High School is said to be the largest and longest mural frieze in the entire South, covering fully 816 square feet.

The Trussville Furnace.
Carrie L. Hill (1875–1957, active in Birmingham 1908–1957). Oil on canvas, 1934. Collection of Patti Mulock, Belleair, Florida. Photograph, 2004 by Lesley R. Collins, Tallassee, Tennessee. Courtesy Birmingham Historical Society.

Southern landscape had long been Carrie Hill's primary source of inspiration. Here, she paints the rusted stoves and cast shed of the Trussville furnace that closed after World War I. The 750-acre site had been recently acquired and designated to become a new federally planned community. Proving unsuitable for farming, it was later developed as the greenbelt community known as Cahaba Village, the core of today's Trussville.

Brother Bryan.
Designed by William Grant (New York, active in Birmingham in the 1930s); carved by George Bridges (1899–1976), Birmingham; dedicated July 29, 1934. Statue, Alabama marble, 1934. Five Points South, Birmingham. Photograph by the Birmingham News, *September 23, 1934. Courtesy BPL Archives.*
[Status: Extant, restored 1983.]

Brother Bryan, the indefatigable local pastor whose religious work touched everyone across the city, is portrayed in his then well-known and characteristic attitude, kneeling to pray. Of his marble statue, Bryan said on dedication day, "It will be out there fighting the devil when I'm gone." According to a letter in the collection of Patrick Cather, federal funds for the commission initially were not sufficient to include a base recommended by the statue's designer. A base has since been added such that the sculpture can be viewed at the appropriate height.

Storybook Mural.
Carrie L. Hill. Mural, oil on canvas, 1937.
Birmingham Public Library East Lake Branch, Birmingham.
Photograph, 2004, by Marc Bondarenko, Courtesy Birmingham Historical Society.
[Status: Extant, restored 1993.]

This full-wall mural, 27 feet long and 9 feet high, was painted for the Children's Reading Room of the East Lake neighborhood library branch. Popular storybook figures, including Prince Charming, Jack and the Bean Stalk, Little Miss Muffet, Old King Cole, the Queen of Hearts, Red Riding Hood and the Wolf, Goldilocks and the Three Bears, Tom Tom the Piper's Son, and three of Snow White's dwarfs escape from the printed page to chat and travel along the road between medieval castles. Carrie Hill's likeness can be recognized as the face of the grand storyteller Mother Goose, *center with pointed black hat.*

Detail, *Storybook Mural.*
Carrie L. Hill.
Photograph, 2004, by Marc Bondarenko, Courtesy Birmingham Historical Society.

ARTISTS ON RELIEF 93

94 DIGGING OUT OF THE GREAT DEPRESSION

Discovery of America Murals.
Frank Hartley Anderson and Martha Fort Anderson (1885–1968). Murals, oil on canvas, 1935–36. Installed in the library of the historic Lakeview School—now Martin Advertising, Inc., Building, Birmingham.
Photographs, 2010, by Frank Jefferson Tombrello, Birmingham Historical Society. Courtesy Birmingham Board of Education and Martin Advertising, Inc.
[Status: Extant, relocated to halls in 1986; several of the original panels are missing, including a map that traced the routes of the explorers.]

These large canvas paintings show the early Viking, Spanish, French, and British explorers. Using prints and photographs then available at the local library, the Anderson team tried to accurately depict the historical figures. It is thought that Frank did the research and sketched the scenes; Martha painted the murals.

Vikings Landing on the Coast of America, *top left.*
Blond men in horned helmets and gold-bronze armor emerge from their sailing craft onto the future American shore. Behind them is a sea of cobalt blue.

Spaniards Arriving at Tikal, *top right.*
Working from a photograph of a restored temple, the Andersons portrayed the grand Mayan pyramid amid banana trees, palmetto fronds, and orchids flanked by an immense stone idol. Two Spanish soldiers are poised in discovery. The scene, however, is fictitious for the Spaniards never actually reached the Mayan city of Tikal.

Christopher Columbus Discovering America, *middle left.*
With his flotilla anchored off this tropical shore, Columbus' outstretched arm and display of Spanish flags and armored soldiers make clear his authority, and that of the Catholic Church, over the submissive native couple.

Columbus Returning to Palos, *middle right.*
European men, women, and children in colorful dress appear in the courtyard of an Italian-style residence as Columbus' ships approach the Spanish port city from which he sailed and to which he returned.

Cabot Claiming America for the British, 1497, *bottom left.*
This scene depicts John Cabot and his son Sebastian landing on the American coast and preparing to run up the British flag.

Jacques Cartier Exploring the St. Lawrence, 1835, *bottom right.*
The vignette shows two natives carefully paddling a canoe, at the bow of which Cartier stands as he patrols the river, brandishing the French flag and laying claim to the region.

Early Settlers Weighing Cotton.
William Sherrod McCall, Jacksonville, Florida.
Mural, oil on canvas, 1939. Montevallo Post Office, Montevallo, Alabama.
Photograph, 2010, by Frank Jefferson Tombrello, Birmingham Historical Society.
[Status: Extant.]

Post Office Murals™ reprinted with the permission of the United States Postal Service. All rights reserved. Written authorization from the Postal Service is required to use, reproduce, post, transmit, distribute, or publicly display these images.

The Montevallo mural reflects the most popular theme of the 1930s post office commissions: Americans at work. Here, men and a woman, with a team of oxen, bear their split-oak baskets of cotton to be weighed for sale. The farm vista fills the background. The Florida artist William Sherrod McCall received the commission for the mural based on designs submitted for a Miami competition. He visited Montevallo and chose the cotton theme, the execution of which greatly pleased the postmaster and the local citizens, who treated him royally, as he commented in his final letter to the federal funding agency.

Detail, *Spirit of Steel*.
Frank Hartley Anderson and Martha Fort Anderson.
Photograph, 2010, by Frank Jefferson Tombrello, Birmingham Historical Society.

Post Office Murals™ reprinted with the permission of the United States Postal Service. All rights reserved. Written authorization from the Postal Service is required to use, reproduce, post, transmit, distribute, or publicly display these images.

The central motif shows a fiery flare of waste gases that lights up area skies, signaling to residents that the works are operating and there will be money in the dinner pails.

Spirit of Steel.
Frank Hartley Anderson and Martha Fort Anderson. Mural, oil on canvas, 1938. Fairfield Post Office, Fairfield, Alabama.
Photograph, 2010, by Frank Jefferson Tombrello, Birmingham Historical Society. [Status: Extant.]

Post Office Murals™ reprinted with the permission of the United States Postal Service. All rights reserved. Written authorization from the Postal Service is required to use, reproduce, post, transmit, distribute, or publicly display these images.

Fairfield postmaster William Gandy chose the story of iron and steelmaking for the mural above his office entrance. In 1938, nearly everyone in Fairfield worked for TCI-U.S. Steel's Fairfield Works or its coal and red ore mines nearby. Fairfield workers produced bar, plate, and structural steel as well as wire and nails at this time. *From left to center*, the mural shows miners within Red Mountain using mechanized drills to knock loose the ore from which iron and steel are made; beside them, workers shovel coal to stoke the boilers that create the steam to provide the blast for the furnaces in which iron is made from the ore. *From right to center*, within a coal mine, shown inside the earth beneath two blast furnaces, miners use a pick and shovel to extract the black gold that fuels the boilers. *In the center*, laborers stoke the boilers, rod the furnaces, and produce the finished rolled steel. As was the convention in such federally funded murals of the 1930s, the workers appear as able-bodied and energetic men who accomplish their tasks with dignity and skill.

ARTISTS ON RELIEF   97

98　DIGGING OUT OF THE GREAT DEPRESSION

Youth's Strife in the Approach to Life's Problems.
Designed by Sidney W. J. Van Sheck (c. 1896–1991), then at Auburn University; painted by Richard Blauvelt Coe; installed by William Grant. Mural frieze, oil on canvas, 1935–38. Auditorium, Woodlawn High School, Birmingham.
Photograph, 2010, by Frank Jefferson Tombrello, Birmingham Historical Society. Courtesy Woodlawn High School.
[Status: Extant, under restoration.]

The Czech-born and European-educated artist and aeronautical engineer Sidney Van Sheck, who in the 1930s served on the interior design faculty at the Alabama Polytechnic Institute (now Auburn University), designed this massive allegory with its 9- and 14-foot heroic figures. A boy and girl, *center*, face life's challenges—industrial exploitation, war, greed, corruption, spiritual intolerance—ultimately triumphing over life's ills to obtain, through agriculture and education, a new social order. In their future ideal life, armed with new scientific and technological improvements such as land terracing, bridges, planning, radio, water power, and speedy transportation, *middle left*—they forsake industrial life and support themselves through agricultural pursuit, *left*. Well schooled and intellectually sharpened by superb teachers and exposure to the arts, *right*, the boy and girl prosper with their improved spiritual and intellectual guidance.

    A motto crafted by Van Sheck, now painted over, originally surmounted the Woodlawn mural: "Gloried be they who forsaking unjust riches strive in fulfillment of humble tasks for peace, culture, and equality of all mankind."

Detail, *Youth's Strife in the Approach to Life's Problems*.
Sidney W. J. Van Sheck and Richard Blauvelt Coe.
Photograph, 2010, by Frank Jefferson Tombrello, Birmingham Historical Society. Courtesy Woodlawn High School.

Historical Panorama of Alabama Agriculture.
Designed by John Augustus Walker, Mobile, Alabama; painted by Walker and Richebourg Gaillard Jr., Mobile, Alabama. Ten panels, tempera on canvas, 1939. Created for the Alabama Cooperative Extension Service Exhibition, Alabama State Fair, Birmingham, October 1939.
Photographs, 2006, Courtesy Alabama Cooperative Extension System.
[Status: Extant, cleaned and remounted, 1985; ownership transferred to the Jule Collins Smith Museum of Fine Art, Auburn, Alabama, 2010.]

Funded by the WPA, Mobile muralist John Augustus Walker created these panels for installation at the Alabama State Fair in Birmingham. Commissioned by the Extension Service of the Alabama Polytechnic Institute (now Auburn University), they tell the story of Alabama agriculture from its origins in the cultivation of corn by indigenous people to the arrival of federal programs of the 1930s advocating scientific and improved practices. Measuring roughly 5 x 7 feet each, the murals were displayed in the agricultural pavilion at the fair and later traveled to other state fairs before being retired to the attic of the extension service. There, in the early 1980s, they were rediscovered and subsequently cleaned, repaired, and briefly exhibited. They were rediscovered again in 2006, researched, and displayed during Auburn University's sesquicentennial celebration.

ARTISTS ON RELIEF 101

Four Panels, *Historical Panorama of Alabama Agriculture.*
John Augustus Walker, 1939.

These bright and cheery murals reveal the philosophical underpinnings of federal agriculture reform. Through the outreach efforts of the Extension Service of the Alabama Polytechnic Institute and the U.S. Department of Agriculture, assisted by the State Agricultural Experimental Station, farmers will plant several cash crops (not just cotton) and will raise

livestock, poultry, and trees, thereby receiving multiple incomes and becoming self-sustaining, as well as wiser and better businessmen who will also protect their soil. In "Our Agriculture and Our Fair," P. O. Davis, Extension Service Director, states the service's intent to reveal "these important facts" to the thousands of fairgoers and to offer them "a vision of the future" for which "we are building Alabama into a better and more prosperous State."

Chapter Eight
On Stage:
The Federal Theatre Project (FTP)

Operating nationally from 1935 to 1939, the WPA's Federal Theatre Project (FTP) pursued the goals of employing theatre workers—actors, directors, technicians, and writers—and bringing affordable dramatic entertainment to everyday Americans. Headed by Vassar theatre professor Hallie Flanagan, the program also sought to encourage the development of plays by local authors on local topics in places where little or no professional theatre existed.

Coordinated from Washington, theatre companies operated in 22 states and 40 cities. In Alabama, the project was sponsored by the State Park and Recreation Board and was headed by John McGee, former director of the Birmingham Little Theatre. A total of $55,000 was allocated to the Alabama project.

Two units operated in Birmingham: the "senior," or white, unit and the "junior," or Negro, unit, the latter the only federally supported African-American theater unit in the Deep South. (The two other Negro units in the Southern Region operated at Durham and Raleigh in North Carolina.) Birmingham was also home to the Southern Play Bureau, which solicited and reviewed script submissions for the region's units, arranged travel, disbursed funds, and provided other administrative support.

In addition to producing stage plays, the Birmingham project hosted "demonstration" workshops, produced radio broadcasts, and toured the state with some productions. The FTP also offered free classes in acting, pantomime, comedy, theatre history, playwriting, lighting and staging, fencing, music, dance, and ballet. The Federal Theatre Singers of Birmingham's Negro unit, overseen by local choir director Harold White McCoo, had their own 30-minute radio show, in addition to performing in each of that unit's stage productions.

Prohibited by a City of Birmingham ordinance from sharing the same performance space as the white unit, the Negro unit operated at the Municipal Auditorium and Industrial High School. With an initial allocation of $5,000, the group's cast included Russell Veal, an experienced actor trained in Birmingham, and soloist Lillie Mae Littlejohn. Its productions, under the guidance of local director Clyde Limbaugh, ranged from stereotypical depictions of African-American life in the South (*Accident Policy* and *Home in Glory*) to plays that sought to

Home in Glory Poster.
Play poster, Birmingham Federal Theatre Project, 1936.
Courtesy Federal Theatre Project Materials Collection, Special Collections and Archives, George Mason University Libraries.

portray the black scene with realism. One example of the latter, Harold Courlander's *Swamp Mud*, used the plight of convict road crews in Georgia as a metaphor for the oppressive circumstances of Southern blacks. (Courlander later would sue, and successfully settle with, *Roots* author Alex Haley for plagiarizing his 1967 novel *The African*.)

The Negro unit's most ambitious production was an "allegory with music" called *Great Day*, the script of which is now lost. Local black playwright Morrison Wood's drama begins in 4500 B.C. in the jungles of Nigeria and follows a tribal prophet and a warrior chief turned slave through the Civil War to the Depression, exploring the subjects of slavery, social change, and black leadership.

Riot Scene from the Atlanta Production of *Altars of Steel*.
Photograph, 1937. Set design by Joseph Lentz.
Courtesy Federal Theatre Project Photographs Collection, Special Collections and Archives, George Mason University Libraries.

Birmingham's white unit performed under the direction of Verner Haldene, of the Montgomery Little Theatre, at the famed Jefferson Theatre at 1710 Second Avenue, producing a total of nine plays during 1936. The group employed 63 workers, including professionals Amasa Windham and Sallie Lee Woodall of the Birmingham Little Theatre and Clyde Waddell of the Walter Ambler Stock Company. The project's high point was the dramatization of *It Can't Happen Here*, which opened simultaneously at 22 federal theatres across the country on October 27, 1936, and was seen by half a million people. Based on a novel by Sinclair Lewis, the play portrays the United States under the control of a fascist dictatorship.

The *Birmingham News* published the work in installments leading up to the play's opening. Among the other plays produced by the senior unit were a "rousing" melodrama (*After Dark*), a locally authored comedy (*Mr. Petruchio*), a satire on public education (*Chalk Dust*), and a courtroom drama by Ayn Rand (*The Night of January 16th*).

One of the most widely seen and discussed plays of the Federal Theatre Project was *Altars of Steel*, an original drama developed by the Birmingham project. The play depicts the struggle between management and labor at a Birmingham steel mill that is acquired by "United Steel," a national company based in the northern United States. A thinly disguised reference to the acquisition of the locally owned Tennessee Coal and Iron Company (TCI) by U.S. Steel, the play features 21 staged deaths, a workers' riot, and an explosion at the mill. Written under the pseudonym Thomas Hall-Rogers, the play is often attributed to local newspaperman John Temple Graves II. However, one recent researcher asserts that the true playwright was Josiah Bancroft, a physiotherapist at the TCI Hospital (later Lloyd Noland Hospital) in Fairfield[1].

Altars of Steel received several public readings in Birmingham and was in rehearsal for a January 1937 opening when the city's theatre project was shut down. Funding cuts, poor attendance, and the lack of qualified theatre professionals and quality scripts contributed to the decision to close the Birmingham units. Picked up by the Atlanta group, *Altars of Steel* premiered on March 29, 1937, and quickly became one of the most discussed Southern plays of the 1930s. Hallie Flanagan described the play as "the most important Southern production." Critics described it as dangerous and inflammatory—too controversial, perhaps, for Birmingham.

Following the demise of the Negro unit, funding for its choir was continued under the WPA's recreation program, and efforts subsequently shifted toward support of recreational activities for the city's African Americans, a cause championed by local park board representative Laura Sharp.

The Federal Theatre Project in Birmingham represents a remarkable, if brief, experiment in Southern regional theatre. Through it, both white and especially black emerging artists gained a venue to explore cultural, social, and economic themes and gave many the opportunity to experience live theatre for the first time.

[1] Osborne, Elizabeth Ann. *Staging the People: Revising and Reenvisioning Community in the Federal Theatre Project.* College Park, MD: University of Maryland, 2007. http://hdl.handle.net/1903/6858.

Production	Author	Dates (# of performances)	Attendance
Home in Glory	Clyde Limbaugh	April 16–17, 1936 (2)	1,617
Swamp Mud	Harold Courlander	July 11, 1936 (1)	630
Accident Policy	Arthur Aker	July 31–August 3, 1936 (2)	230
Great Day	Morrison Wood	October 8, 1936	——

Performance List, Birmingham Federal Theatre Stock Unit (Negro).
Source: *John Russell Poole,* The Federal Theatre Project in Georgia and Alabama: An Historical Analysis of Government Theatre in the Deep South. *Ph.D. Dissertation, University of Georgia, Athens, 1995.*

Production	Author	Dates (# of performances)	Attendance
After Dark	Dion Boucicault	May 12–16, 1936 (6)	713
Mr. Petruchio	Amasa B. Windham & Mary Mabry	May 19–23, 1936 (6)	1,057
The Spider	Fulton Oursler & Lowell Brentano	May 26– June 6, 1936 (12)	2,028
Let Who Will Be Clever	Alden Nash	June 3–9, 1936 (6)	1,134
Chalk Dust	Harold A. Clarke & Maxwell Nurnberg	June 16–Sept. 21, 1936 (12)	1,640
It Can't Happen Here	Sinclair Lewis & John Moffitt	Oct. 27–Dec. 2, 1936 (12)	2,024
The Night of January 16th	Ayn Rand	Nov. 10–14, 1936 (6)	1,198
Distant Drums	Dan Totheroh	Nov. 17–21, 1936 (6)	642
American Holiday	Edwin Barker & Albert Barker	Dec. 27–31, 1936 (6)	819

Performance List, Birmingham Federal Theatre Stock Unit (White).
Source: *John Russell Poole,* The Federal Theatre Project in Georgia and Alabama: An Historical Analysis of Government Theatre in the Deep South. *Ph.D. Dissertation, University of Georgia, Athens, 1995.*

FEDERAL THEATER DRAMA IS PRAISED
"The Night Of January 16th" Given Unqualified Okeh By Reviewer

For genuine interest and entertainment, "The Night of January 16th," current Broadway theatrical hit offered here by the Federal Theater project, is hard to beat. The production opened last night for a five-day run.

It's a murder mystery, not of the weird, gruesome type that for a number of years took first place among dramatic productions, but rather one which depends upon an intricate weaving and interweaving of fact and fancy, plot and counter-plot, to create the problem upon which the spectator may draw his own conclusions as to the guilt or innocence of the principals.

The play deals with the death of a great financier. The death at first is believed to be suicide, but soon develops into murder. The story is told entirely from the witness stand in the trial of the central character, Karen Andre, mistress of the dead financier. The jury for the trial is drawn from the audience and reaches its conclusions from the facts presented by prosecution and defense counsel.

Last night's performance was sparkling, and individual performances of the federal players were masterly and convincing. Especially those of Miss Helen Stringfellow (Karen Andre) and Sally Lee Woodall as Nancy Lee Faulkner, legitimate wife of the dead Faulkner. Miss Stringfellow brought to the role of the Andre woman much that the creator of the character sought to give it. The hushed suspense of the audience while she gave her testimony from the stand was a silent tribute to her interpretation of the role.

Clyde Waddell, as the prosecuting attorney, turned in his usually good performance, while Lydia Woodstock, as a Swedish maid, and Craig Neslo, as a private detective, took care of the comedy relief in a business-like manner. Hal Brown, whose interpretation of Deramus in a previous federal project, was a high mark in histrionics, turns around in this performance to create a character that in many respects is a direct opposite and does it in an equally convincing manner.

There's only one way to know about what happened on "The Night of January 16th," and that is to see the performance. This reviewer feels he will be betraying no friendships nor making no enemies in recommending it as a rattling good bit of entertainment—WILLIAM M. HINDS.

Review of *The Night of January 16th*.
Birmingham News, *November 11, 1936. Clipping Files (Birmingham – Theatres – Federal Project), BPL Southern History.*

CAST CHOSEN IN NEGRO PROJECT
First Play Takes Actors From WPA Rolls; Parts Are Assigned

Twenty-six Birmingham Negroes—whose jobs used to range from washing clothes to teaching school—have suddenly become actors for the play, "Home in Glory," to be presented in April by the Negro Repertory Theater, first of the Federal theater projects here.

Every afternoon at the colored Y. W. C. A. the group, selected from the rolls of Works Progress Administration, rehearses the new roles. A former washwoman was discovered to have the acting ability which put her in the leading part of Emma.

The play of Negro life in Shelby County was written as a "symphonic drama" by Clyde Limbaugh, supervisor and director of the project. A chorus of 100 voices will weave spirituals into the plot.

"This play will be a new start toward developing native drama among Negroes," said Mr. Limbaugh.

"Ever since I helped with the production of 'Roll, Sweet Chariot' at Legion Field last year, I've been eager to see a further opportunity given to Negroes to express themselves through drama."

Mr. Limbaugh interviewed more than 100 WPA workers before choosing the cast for the play. The new actors don't know the exact date or building where they will make their appearance in April—but meanwhile they are diligently rehearsing the play. In it Emma holds the other characters at bay with her outbursts of religious fervor—amplified by the chanting of such songs as "Certainly, Lord" and "Look Away."

Mr. Limbaugh's appointment to direct the Negro project here was announced by John McGee, regional director for the Federal theater project.

"Cast Chosen in Negro Project."
Birmingham Post, *March 31, 1936. Clipping Files (Birmingham – Theatres – Federal Project), BPL Southern History.*

Chapter Nine
Digging Up the Past:
Advances in Archaeology

With its moderate climate and an available large, mostly unskilled labor force, the Southeast proved fertile ground for intensive archaeological investigation of prehistoric Native American sites. During the 1930s, field teams sponsored by the Federal Emergency Relief Administration (FERA), Civil Works Administration (CWA), Civilian Conservation Corps (CCC), and Works Progress Administration (WPA) excavated sites throughout Alabama, uncovering thousands of artifacts that continue to merit study today. The people who created and sustained the sites as early as 5000 B.C. left no written records. Hence, it is through archeological evidence their story continues to be pieced together and told.

Dr. Walter B. Jones, state geologist and director of the Alabama Museum of Natural History, oversaw expeditions at Bessemer and Moundville, where Native Americans of the Mississippian mound-building culture lived. Museum archaeologist David L. DeJarnette conducted the excavations. At Bessemer, three large earthen mounds and an adjoining village area were excavated, using labor and supplies provided by the CWA and WPA. Excavation of the Moundville site, containing 26 large earthen mounds just south of Tuscaloosa, took place from 1933 to 1941. The Moundville museum was also established here in 1939 with the aid of the CCC (see photographs, page 29). At its peak in 1350, the complex Moundville site was the largest center of population in the future United States.

Under DeJarnette's direction, large-scale excavations were also conducted in the Guntersville, Pickwick, and Wheeler basins of the Tennessee River, prior to flooding of these areas for TVA dam construction. A labor force of more than 1,000 CWA and WPA workers here and elsewhere in the Southeast operated under TVA supervision. There were extensive WPA-era excavations in South Alabama as well.

The fruits of the Alabama field work—pottery shards, projectile points, bone fragments, and other objects—were sent to the WPA Central Archaeological Laboratory in Birmingham. Here, under the supervision of lab director Marion Dunlevy and Alabama Museum anthropologist Christine Adcock, artifacts were cleaned, photographed,

General View of Archaeological Excavations, Bessemer Site.
Photograph, October 1, 1939.
Courtesy The University of Alabama Museums, Tuscaloosa, Alabama (21 Je 14).

cataloged, and studied. Workers at the lab reconstructed pottery vessels, restored and documented skeletal material, sketched and categorized artifact forms, and drew maps depicting the distribution of the objects at their original locations.

First Lady Eleanor Roosevelt, in town in November 1938 to attend the inaugural meeting of the Southern Conference for Human Welfare (at which the Birmingham lab exhibited), toured the Central Archaeological Laboratory and was much impressed:

> "It is an extraordinarily interesting project, but what seemed to me remarkable was that this work which requires so much knowledge and skill is being done by WPA workers who never before reconstructed a pottery vase from fragments found in a burial mound, or rearranged the bones of skeletons or reconstituted a skull from a variety of fragments.
>
> ...In other states archaeological projects such as these are carried on through the university laboratories, but in Georgia and Alabama these facilities did not exist, so this laboratory is a rather unique contribution to the education of the state as far as its past is concerned."

Source: Eleanor Roosevelt, "My Day" newspaper column, November 23, 1938, http://www.gwu.edu/~erpapers.

That same month, the Birmingham lab hosted the second meeting of the Southeastern Archaeological Conference, a group formed earlier that year to promote information sharing among excavators in the region and to standardize ceramic types. The lab facility operated from the summer of 1938 until the spring of 1942, when it was closed due to wartime priorities.

The lab's artifacts and records, as well as those from the Moundville site, are now housed at the University of Alabama Museums. The WPA/TVA archeological photographs and field notes are permanently curated for the TVA by the Frank H. McClung Museum at the University of Tennessee, the William S. Webb Museum of Anthropology at the University of Kentucky, and the University of Alabama Museums, with each institution housing approximately 5,000 images for projects within its bounds. The photo archive can be viewed online at *http://diglib.lib.utk.edu/wpa/index.php*. Additional photos, particularly of the Bessemer site, are available through the University of Alabama Museums' Office of Archaeological Research at *http://museums.ua.edu/oar/NEH/index.shtml*.

"Cleaning Artifacts at the Central Archeological Laboratory in Birmingham, Alabama."
Photograph, September 15, 1938, by James R. Foster.
Courtesy The University of Alabama Museums, Tuscaloosa, Alabama (3CAL) (uam02346).

"Artifact Analysis at the Central Archeological Laboratory in Birmingham, Alabama."
Photograph, September 1, 1938, by James R. Foster.
Courtesy The University of Alabama Museums, Tuscaloosa, Alabama (1CAL) (uam01971).

"Drafting at the Central Archeological Laboratory in Birmingham, Alabama."
Photograph, September 1, 1938, by James R. Foster.
Courtesy The University of Alabama Museums, Tuscaloosa, Alabama (4CAL) (uam01973).

"The Central Archeological Laboratory in Birmingham, Alabama houses data regarding Alabama archeology and makes it available to archaeologists all over the United States."
Photograph, September 20, 1938, by James R. Foster.
Courtesy The University of Alabama Museums, Tuscaloosa, Alabama (10CAL) (uam01977).

DIGGING UP THE PAST

Eleanor Roosevelt (*third from left*) visiting Alabama's WPA archaeological laboratory.
Photograph, November 20, 1938, by James R. Foster.
Courtesy The University of Alabama Museums, Tuscaloosa, Alabama (16CAL).

"Exhibit by the Central Archaeological Laboratory at the Conference on Human Welfare on November 20 to 23, 1938, in Birmingham, Alabama."
Interior, Municipal–now Boutwell Auditorium.
Photograph, November 15, 1938, by James R. Foster.
Courtesy The University of Alabama Museums, Tuscaloosa, Alabama (19CAL).

More than 5,000 Southerners met here to explore improving the economy and rigid racial restrictions. When City officials enforced segregated seating, the First Lady moved her chair to the middle of the aisle.

DIGGING UP THE PAST

Chapter Ten
Recording Our Heritage:
The Historic American Buildings Survey (HABS)

The nation's first federal preservation program began in 1933 to document America's architectural heritage. The initial program set up district offices, hired unemployed architects, and sent them out to measure, draw, and photograph pre-1860 structures. Birmingham hosted an early district office.

The founding philosophy of the Historic American Buildings Survey (HABS) was more than just unemployment relief. It noted that comparatively few structures can be saved by extraordinary effort as historic houses and museums or altered and used for new purposes. The founder stated that if "the great number of our interesting and important architectural specimens" must disappear, they could, at least, be recorded through measured drawings and photographs for a national collection.

State Advisory Committees worked with district officers to review the existing literature and other documentation on the historic buildings in their states, to select and rank the buildings for the survey, and to gain the approval of the Washington office.

The HABS collection begun in the 1930s and continued throughout the years by the Washington-based agency is now housed at the Library of Congress, where it is among the most used collections of the library.

Three pre-1860 structures were documented in Birmingham: the Mudd, Walker, and Worthington Houses in the Elyton and Southside areas of the city. The Mudd House is now Arlington Historic House and Garden, a museum of the City of Birmingham. The Walker and Worthington Houses have been demolished. HABS photographer Alex Bush made and captioned the photographs of the three properties on March 4, 1937.

"Front Elevation, William S. Mudd-Robert S. Munger House, built 1842, 331 Cotton Avenue, Elyton."
Photograph by Alex Bush, 1937.
Courtesy Historic American Buildings Survey (HABS)
(HABS ALA37-BIRM, 1-1).
[Status: Preserved and open to the public as Arlington Historic House and Garden, Birmingham.]

RECORDING OUR HERITAGE 115

"Front (North) and West Elevation, Mudd House."
Photograph by Alex Bush, 1937.
Courtesy HABS (HABS ALA 37-BIRM, 1-7).

"Front of Hall (General View), Mudd House."
Photograph by Alex Bush, 1937.
Courtesy HABS (HABS ALA 37-BIRM, 1-10).

"Front (North) and West Elevation, William A. Walker House, built 1848, 200 Broad Street, Elyton."
Photograph by Alex Bush, 1937.
Courtesy HABS (HABS ALA 37-BIRM, 2-1).
[Status: Demolished.]

"Stairwell in Main Hall, Walker House."
Photograph by Alex Bush, 1937.
Courtesy HABS (HABS ALA 37-BIRM, 2-6).

"Looking South at Well, Walker House."
Photograph by Alex Bush, 1937.
Courtesy HABS (HABS ALA 37-BIRM, 2-10).

"Mantel on West Wall of Parlor, Walker House."
Photograph by Alex Bush, 1937.
Courtesy HABS (HABS ALA 37-BIRM, 2-6).

"Front (North) and West Elevation, Benjamin Pinckney Worthington House, Sixth Avenue South."
Photograph by Alex Bush, 1937.
Courtesy HABS (HABS ALA 37-BIRM, 3-1).
[Status: Demolished.]

"Close Up of Main Entrance, Worthington House."
Photograph by Alex Bush, 1937. Courtesy HABS (HABS ALA 37-BIRM, 3-6).

"Stairway to Rear of Main Hall, Worthington House."
Photograph by Alex Bush, 1937. Courtesy HABS (HABS ALA 37-BIRM, 23-7).

"Rear (South) Elevation, Worthington House."
*Photograph by Alex Bush, 1937.
Courtesy HABS (HABS ALA 37-BIRM, 3-2).*

CHAPTER ELEVEN
BUILT TO LAST:
A LEGACY IN STONE AT BIRMINGHAM PARKS

Stonework of the Great Depression appears to seamlessly fit its setting. And there is good reason that it does.

Construction materials were quarried on site by the stone cutters who built park structures—the roads and bridges into the parks, the picnic pavilions and barbecue pits, fish hatcheries and piers, and staircases, cabins, and towers that were popular in the 1930s. Use of local materials cut construction costs and worked well with federal programs such as the Civil Works and Works Progress Administrations (the CWA and the WPA), which provided funds to hire men, not machines or materials.

A City of Birmingham bond issue in 1931 also provided funds to hire unemployed workers to build recreational structures in Birmingham parks, most notably the amphitheatre and shelter house at Avondale Park, then the city's largest park, and a pool house at Ensley Park, then the largest western area park. The CWA funded bridges and drainage improvements at Green Springs Park—today's George Ward Park and shelter and community houses and barbeque pits at Lane Park—today's Birmingham Zoo. WPA workers built an arboretum at Lane Park and developed the fish hatchery ponds here; built bridges and fishing piers at East Lake Park; and completed the moving and erecting of the industrial city's symbol, the mammoth cast iron statue of Vulcan atop a monumental column within the new Red Mountain park overlooking the city of Birmingham.

Using stone that was available on site is mentioned frequently in write-ups of 1930s projects. Also noted is the reuse of stone, brick, and lumber from demolished older structures, such as obsolete schools, coke ovens, and even the former Jefferson County Courthouse and the Loveman's Department store.

This collection of photographs of stone structures in Birmingham parks was made and printed in 2003 by students in Professor Pam Venz's January Term Photographic Studio at Birmingham-Southern College. Birmingham Historical Society provided the research and guidance for documentation of this remarkable legacy.

Swimming Pool-Now Western Maintenance Division, Ensley Park, *above.*
Built 1931 with funds from a City of Birmingham bond issue for parks.
Photograph by Charles Horn, 2003. Courtesy Birmingham Historical Society.

Shelter House-Now Picnic Pavilion, Avondale Park, *right.*
Built 1931 with funds from a City of Birmingham bond issue for parks.
Photograph by Andrew Ryan, 2003. Courtesy Birmingham Historical Society.

Entrance Gate and Bench, Avondale Park.
Built 1931 with funds from a City of Birmingham bond issue for parks.
Photograph by Andrew Ryan, 2003. Courtesy Birmingham Historical Society.

Amphitheatre Stage and Staging Pavilions, Avondale Park.
Designed by landscape architect Rubee J. Pearse and built 1931 with funds from a City of Birmingham bond issue for parks.
Photograph by Andrew Ryan, 2003. Courtesy Birmingham Historical Society.

Amphitheatre Seating, Avondale Park.
Designed by landscape architect Rubee J. Pearse and built 1931 with funds from a City of Birmingham bond issue for parks.
Photograph by Andrew Ryan, 2003. Courtesy Birmingham Historical Society.

Drainage Ditch, Green Springs Park-Now George Ward Park. *Built 1933-34 with funds from the Civil Works Administration. Photograph by Adam Colbert, 2003. Courtesy Birmingham Historical Society.*

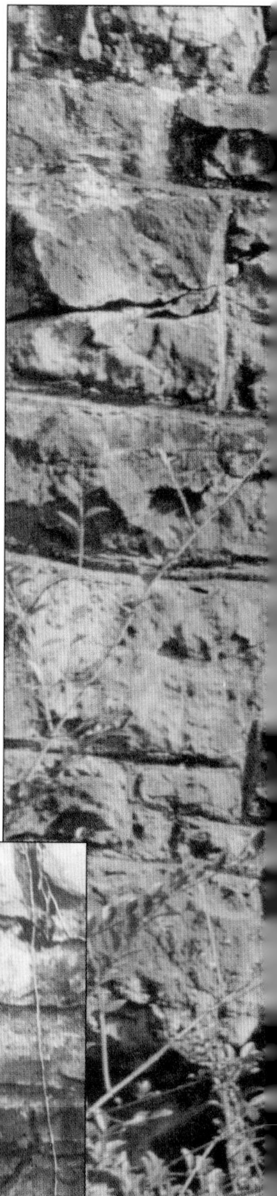

Bridges, Green Springs Park–Now George Ward Park, *left and above.*
Built 1933-34 with funds from the Civil Works Administration.
Photograph by Adam Colbert, 2003. Courtesy Birmingham Historical Society.

Community House, Lane Park–Now the Lodge at the Birmingham Zoo.
Built 1933-34 with funds from the Civil Works Administration.
Photograph by Annette Kittrell, 2003. Courtesy Birmingham Historical Society.

Shelter House, Lane Park-Now Picnic Pavilion at the Birmingham Zoo.
Built 1933-34 with funds from the Civil Works Administration.
Photograph by Booth Wilson, 2003. Courtesy Birmingham Historical Society.

Barbecue Pit at the Community House, Lane Park-Now the Lodge at the Birmingham Zoo.
Built 1933-34 with funds from the Civil Works Administration. Photograph by Jamie Neal, 2003. Courtesy Birmingham Historical Society.

Fish Hatchery Basins, Lane Park-Now the Birmingham Zoo Ponds.
Built 1936-1937 by the Works Progress Administration.
Photograph by Booth Wilson, 2003. Courtesy Birmingham Historical Society.

Staircase, Fish Hatchery Basins, Lane Park-Now the Birmingham Zoo.
Built 1936-1937 by the Works Progress Administration.
Photograph by Annette Kittrell, 2003. Courtesy Birmingham Historical Society.

BUILT TO LAST 129

Entrance Gate, Vulcan Park.
Built 1936-1938 by the Works Progress Administration. Photograph by Charles Horn, 2003. Courtesy Birmingham Historical Society.

Staircase from Streetcar Stop, Vulcan Park, *left.*
Built 1936-1938 by the Works Progress Administration. Photograph by Charles Horn, 2003. Courtesy Birmingham Historical Society.

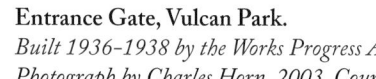

Index

A
Abercrombie, Joseph H., 86
Adcock, Christine, 108
Agricultural Adjustment Act (AAA), 1
airports, 10, 11, 76, 77
Alabama (Bankhead) National Forest, 19, 21, 27
Alabama Cooperative Extension Service, vi, 84, 100–103
Alabama Museum of Natural History, 108
Alabama State Fair, 100
alphabet agencies, 1
Altars of Steel, 105–106
American Guide Series, 3
Anderson, Frank Hartley, 88, 90, 94–95, 97
Anderson, Martha Fort, 88, 90, 94–95, 97
archaeology, 108–113
Arlington Historic House and Garden, 114–116
art programs. *See* Federal art programs
athletic fields, 14–16

B
Bancroft, Josiah, 106
Bankhead, John Jr., 1, 38
Bankhead Farms, 38
Bankhead National Forest. *See* Alabama (Bankhead) National Forest
beautification efforts, vi, 84–87
Beecher, John, 54
Bessemer, viii, 12, 16, 19, 29, 34, 43, 76–77, 108–109
Birmingham
  bond issue of 1931, vi, 120–123
  city shops and garage, 6, 76
  conditions in the 1930s, ix
  federal expenditures, ix
  Southside jail, 76
  worker housing, 40–49
Birmingham Municipal Airport, 10, 11, 76, 77
Birmingham Municipal Auditorium, 77, 104, 112–113
Birmingham–The Industrial City Beautiful, 86
Birmingham Zoo. *See* Lane Park
Bridges, George, 92
Brooks, Marion Thomas, 84, 85
Brookside, 49, 54
Bureau of Air Commerce, 2
Byrne, T. K., 85, 86

C
Cahaba Village (Trussville). *See* Slagheap Village (Trussville)
Central Archaeological Laboratory, 108–113
Cheaha State Park, 23, 30–31, 35
Chewacla State Park, 37
Civil Aeronautics Authority (CAA), 2

Civil Works Administration
  athletic fields and other school improvements, 14
  federal expenditure, ix, 5
  Jefferson County projects site map, 4–5
  opening meeting in Birmingham, ix
  park improvements, 12–13, 120, 124–127
  projects, 2, 4–17, 108
  public facility improvements, 6
  and Public Works of Art Project, 88
  Report of the Civil Works Administration, Jefferson County Division, 5
  storm water improvements, 10–11
  street and road improvements, 7
Civilian Conservation Corps
  at Alabama (Bankhead) National Forest, 19, 21, 27
  camp life, 20–22
  Camp F-1 (Moulton), 21
  Camp F-2 (Danville), 19
  Camp F-5 (Double Springs), 22
  Camp F-6 (Heflin), 19
  Camp F-7 (Chandler Springs), 19, 21, 22, 26
  Camp F-9 (Andalusia), 24, 26, 28
  Camp P-54 (Brewton), 20, 22
  Camp P-81 (Bessemer), 19
  Camp S-52 (Chunchula), 27
  Camp SP-7, 24
  Camp SP-8 (Bessemer), 19, 29
  Camp SP-15, 29
  Camp TVA P-13 (Huntsville), 22
  at Cheaha State Park, 23, 30–31, 35
  at Chewacla State Park, 37
  at Conecuh National Forest, 23, 24, 25, 26, 27, 28
  enrollee pay, 19
  fire suppression and forest regeneration, 24–26
  forest work, 23
  map, 18
  at Mound State Monument, 29, 36
  at Oak Mountain State Park, 34
  at Open Pond Recreational Area, 28
  projects, x, 1, 18–37, 108
  recreational areas, 28
  road and bridge building, 27
  state expenditure, 18
  at Talladega National Forest, 19, 24, 26, 30–31
  at Weogufka State Park, 23
Civilian Conservation Corps in Alabama: A Great and Lasting Good, vi
Coe, Richard Blauvelt, 88–89, 98–99
Commodity Credit Corporation, 1
Conecuh National Forest, 23, 24, 25, 26, 27, 28
Courlander, Harold, 104
Crape Myrtle Trail, 86–87

D
Davis, P. O., 103
DeBardeleben, Charles, 64
DeJarnette, David L., 29, 36, 108
Dunlevy, Marion, 108

E
East Lake Library mural, 93
Elliott, Hannah, 88
Elyton Village housing project, x, 69–70
Emergency Banking Act, 1
Evans, Walker, v, x, 40

F
Fair Labor Standards Act, 3
Fairfield, 10, 54, 55, 76, 87, 90, 91, 97
Fairfield post office mural, 90, 91, 97
Farm Credit Administration (FCA), 1
Farm Security Administration (FSA), v, 2
federal art programs, 2, 88–107
Federal Art Project (FAP), 88–90
Federal Aviation Authority (FAA), 2
Federal Communications Commission (FCC), 2
Federal Deposit Insurance Corporation (FDIC), 1
Federal Emergency Relief Administration (FERA), 1, 108
Federal Housing Administration (FHA), 2, 66
Federal Music Project, 3, 90
Federal Theatre Project (FTP), 3, 90, 104–107
Federal Theatre Singers, 104
Federal Writers' Project (FWP), 3, 90
Fischer, Homer S., 84
Fitzpatrick, John Kelly, 88
Flanagan, Hallie, 104, 106
Flechner, Robert, 29
Foster, Charles, 21

G
Gaillard, Richebourg Jr., 100–103
Gandy, William, 97
Gardendale Tract, 56–63
Gee's Bend Farms, 38
Gladner, Henry, 34
Grant, William, 88, 92, 98–99
Graves, John Temple II, 106
Graymont National Guard Armory, 76, 77
Great Day, 104
greenbelt communities, 64
Greenwood subsistence homestead, x, 38, 52–53, 74
Greer, D. H., 52, 56, 64

H
Haley, Alex, 104
Hall-Rogers, Thomas, 106
Hibben, Thomas Jr., v, x, 40, 58

Hill, Carrie L., 88, 92, 93
Hillman Hospital Outpatient Clinic, 78
Historic American Buildings Survey (HABS), v, 2, 114–119
Historical Panorama of Alabama Agriculture, vi, 100–103
Historical Records Survey (HRS), 90
Holmquist, William, 52, 56
Holt, Thad, 88
Home Owners' Loan Corporation (HOLC), 1
Homewood, 2, 8, 12, 82, 83
hospitals and clinics, 2, 76, 78, 79
housing, 38–71, 76
Housing Act of 1937, 66
Housing Authority of the Birmingham District, 76
housing projects
  Central City, x
  Elyton Village, x, 66, 69–70
  federal expenditures, x, 3
  Smithfield Court, x, 66–68
  Southtown, x

I
Index to Alabama Biography, 3
Industrial Waterworks System, ix, 76
Inland Lake, ix
It Can't Happen Here, 105

J
Jefferson County
  tax assessor records, 76
  WPA administrative projects, 76
  WPA employment, ix
Jefferson Hospital, x, 78
Jefferson Tower. *See* Jefferson Hospital
Jemison, Robert Jr., 2, 64, 66, 85
Jones Archaeological Museum, x
Jones, James M. "Jimmie," x, 66
Jones, Walter B., 29, 36, 108

K
Kessler, William, 64

L
Lakeview School murals, 94–95
Lane Park, 13, 80, 86, 120, 126–129
Lewisburg, 45, 49
Lies, J. F., 64
Limbaugh, Clyde, 104
Littlejohn, Lillie Mae, 104

M
Marshall, Roy S., 85
Martin, Sentell, 19
McCall, William Sherrod, 96
McCoo, Harold White, 104
McGee, John, 104
McWane, James R., vi
Montevallo post office mural, 90, 91, 96
Mound State Monument, 29, 36

Moundville, 29, 108
Moundville Archaeological Museum, x, 29, 36, 108
Mount Olive subsistence homestead, v, x, 38, 56–63
Mudd House, William S., 114–116
Munger House, Robert S., 114–116
Municipal Auditorium. *See* Birmingham Municipal Auditorium
Municipal Stadium, 80
murals
   Alabama Cooperative Extension Service, 100–103
   in Alabama post offices, 90–91
   East Lake Library, 93
   Fairfield post office, 90, 91, 97
   Lakeview School, 94–95
   Montevallo post office, 90, 91, 96
   Woodlawn High School, 98–99
Muscoda, 43, 48
Mydans, Carl, v, x, 40, 50

N
national forests
   Alabama (Bankhead), 19, 21
   Conecuh, 23, 24, 25, 26, 27, 28
   Talladega, 19, 24, 26, 30–31
National Guard armories, 76, 77
National Industrial Recovery Act, 1
National Labor Relations Board (NLRB), 2
National Youth Administration (NYA), 2, 83
Natural Resources Conservation Service, 1
New Deal landmarks in Birmingham area, x
North Birmingham, 7

O
Oak Mountain State Park, x, 34, 80
Open Pond Recreational Area, 28

P
Palmerdale subsistence homestead, x, 38, 50–51
Park Lane Apartments (Mountain Brook), 66, 71
Parks, city
   ACIPCO Park, 80
   Avondale, 80, 120–123
   Central Park, 80
   CWA work at, 12–13
   East Lake, 80, 120
   Ensley Park, 120
   Green Springs (George Ward) Park, 11, 120, 124–125
   Hawkins Park, 80
   Homewood Park, 12
   Lane Park, 13, 80, 120, 126–129
   McLendon Park, 76, 77, 80
   Municipal (Roosevelt) Park, 12
   Overton Park (Homewood), 2
   Vulcan Park, 80, 81, 120, 130
   Woodrow Wilson, 80
   WPA work at, 80
parks, state
   brochure, 32–33
   Cheaha State Park, 23, 30–31, 35
   Chewacla State Park, 37
   Oak Mountain State Park, x, 34
   Weogufka State Park, 23

Pearse, Rubee J., 122–123
post office murals, 90, 91
Prairie Farms, 38
public housing. *See* housing projects
Public Works Administration (PWA), ix, 1, 3, 66–70, 78
Public Works of Art Project (PWAP), 2
Puerto Rico Reconstruction Administration (PRRA), 3
Public Works of Art Project (PWAP), 88

R
rammed earth housing, v, 58–63
Ramsay, Erskine, 38, 85
Recreational Demonstration Areas (RDAs), x, 3
Reconstruction Finance Corporation, 1
Redmont Gardens (Mountain Brook), 66
Republic Steel, 42
Resettlement Administration, x, 2, 34, 38, 50, 64
Resettlement Administration photographers, v, x, 38–65
Roberts Field, 76
Roebuck Springs Golf Course, 80
Roosevelt, Eleanor, x, 21, 66, 109, 113
Roosevelt, Franklin D., ix, 18
Rothstein, Arthur, v, x, 40, 50, 52, 54, 56, 64
Rural Electrification Administration (REA), 3
Rushing, Brian, 34

S
Schools
   17th Avenue School, 83
   30th Street School, 83
   Alabama Boy's Industrial School, 83
   Alabama State Training School for Girls, 16, 87
   Alley School, 83
   Baker School, 83
   Barrett School, 83
   Belview Heights School, 83
   Councill School, 82, 83
   Curry School, 83
   CWA school improvements, 14–17
   Ensley High School, 14
   Fairfield High School, 83
   Gardendale School, 83
   Gate City School, 83
   Gibson School, 83
   Gorgas School, 83
   Graymont Elementary School, 83
   Henley School, 92
   Hooper City School, 83
   Huffman School, 83
   Hueytown School, 14
   Industrial High School, 83, 104
   Inglenook School, 83
   Lakeview School, 83, 94–95
   Lewisburg School, 15, 76
   Lincoln Elementary School, 79, 83
   McAdory High School, 82, 83
   Minnie Holman School, 83
   Mortimer Jordan High School, 17
   Ramsay High School, 82, 83
   Riley School, 83

Rosedale School (Homewood), 82, 83
Snow Rogers School, 83
South Highlands School, 83
Springdale School, 17
Tarrant City School, 15, 87
Tarrant High School, 83
Tuggle School, 83
Warrior High School, 17, 83
West End High School, 83
Wilson School, 83
Woodlawn High School, 83, 87, 92, 98–99
Section of Fine Arts, 2, 90
Section of Painting and Sculpture, 2, 90
Securities and Exchange Commission (SEC), 2
sewing rooms, 78, 79
Shades Valley Sewage Disposal Plant, 6
Sky Way Motor Way, 30–31, 35
Skyline Farms, 38
Slagheap Village (Trussville), x, 38, 64–65, 92
Sloss-Sheffield Steel and Iron Company, 45
Slossfield Clinic, 2, 76, 79
Slossfield Negro Youth Training Center, 76
Slossfield Community Center, 76, 77
slum clearance, 66
Smithfield Court housing project, x, 66–68
Snow Rogers Community Center, 2, 76
Social Security Board–Administration, 3
Soil Erosion Service (SES), 1
Southeastern Archaeological Conference, 110
Southern Conference for Human Welfare, 109, 112–113
Southern Play Bureau, 104
Southtown housing project, x
Springdale School, 17
St. Nicholas Russian Orthodox Church, 49
state parks. *See* parks, state
subsistence homesteads
   Bankhead Farms, 38
   federal expenditures, 38
   Gee's Bend Farms, 38
   Greenwood, x, 38
   Mount Olive, v, x, 38, 56–63
   Palmerdale, x, 38
   Prairie Farms, 38
   program, 1, 38
   rammed earth construction, 58–63
   Skyline Farms, 38
   Trussville, x, 38, 92

T
Talladega National Forest, 19, 24, 26, 30–31
TCI–U.S. Steel, 40, 42, 43, 44, 97, 106
Tarrant, 6, 9, 15
theatre. *See* Federal Theatre Project (FTP)
Thomas, 42
Tennessee Valley Authority (TVA), vi, 1, 108
Tranquility Lake, x, 3

Trussville, x, 38, 64–65
Tuberculosis Sanatorium (Homewood), 78–79

U
unemployment, ix
United States Department of Agriculture (USDA), 1
United States Department of Housing and Urban Development (HUD), 2
United States Housing Authority (USHA), 3
United States Treasury Department, 2, 88, 90
University of Alabama Medical Center, x

V
Van Sheck, Sidney, 88, 98–99
Veal, Russell, 104
Vulcan Monument, 80, 81, 87, 120, 130

W
Walker, John Augustus, 100–103
Walker House, William A., 117–118
Warrior airport, 76
Warrior High School, 17
Weogufka State Park, 23
Williams, Aubrey, 2
Windham, Amasa, 105
Wolcott, Marion Post, v, x, 40
Wood, Morrison, 104
Woodall, Sallie Lee, 104, 105
Woodlawn High School mural, 98–99
Works Progress Administration (WPA)
   archaeology projects, 108–113
   art project, 88–92
   aviation projects, 76–77
   beautification projects, vi, 84–87
   Central Archaeological Laboratory, 108
   described, ix, 2, 73
   drainage and sewer projects, 74–75
   employment in Jefferson County, ix
   expenditures, 73
   Industrial Waterworks, 76
   military projects, 76
   park projects, 80, 120, 128–130
   projects card file, v
   projects in Birmingham and Jefferson County, 72–83, 87
   public administration projects, 76
   public building and grounds projects, 76–77
   public health and welfare projects, 78–79
   school projects, 82–83
   street, road, and highway projects, 74–75
   theatre project, 104–107
Works Project Administration. *See* Works Progress Administration (WPA)
Worthington House, Benjamin Pinckney, 118–119
WPA/TVA Archaeological Photographs, vi, 108–113
Wylam, 54, 55